Safeguarding Children, Young People and Families

Sara Miller McCune founded SAGE Publishing in 1965 to support the dissemination of usable knowledge and educate a global community. SAGE publishes more than 1,000 journals and over 800 new books each year, spanning a wide range of subject areas. Our growing selection of library products includes archives, data, case studies and video. SAGE remains majority owned by our founder and after her lifetime will become owned by a charitable trust that secures the company's continued independence.

Los Angeles | London | New Delhi | Singapore | Washington DC | Melbourne

Safeguarding Children, Young People and Families

VIDA DOUGLAS and JULIE FOURIE

Series Editor: Keith Brown

 Learning Matters

Learning Matters
A SAGE Publishing Company
1 Oliver's Yard
55 City Road
London EC1Y 1SP

SAGE Publications Inc.
2455 Teller Road
Thousand Oaks, California 91320

SAGE Publications India Pvt Ltd
B 1/I 1 Mohan Cooperative Industrial Area
Mathura Road
New Delhi 110 044

SAGE Publications Asia-Pacific Pte Ltd
3 Church Street
#10-04 Samsung Hub
Singapore 049483

Editor: Kate Keers
Development editor: Sarah Turpie
Senior project editor: Chris Marke
Project management: TNQ Technologies
Marketing manager: Camille Richmond
Cover design: Sheila Tong
Typeset by: TNQ Technologies
Printed in the UK

Library of Congress Control Number: 2021942055

British Library Cataloguing in Publication Data

A catalogue record for this book is available from the British Library

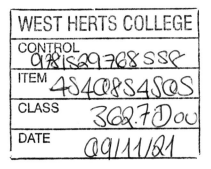
ISBN 978-1-5297-6856-5
ISBN 978-1-5297-6855-8 (pbk)

At SAGE we take sustainability seriously. Most of our products are printed in the UK using responsibly sourced papers and boards. When we print overseas we ensure sustainable papers are used as measured by the PREPS grading system. We undertake an annual audit to monitor our sustainability.

Contents

About the Authors

Vida Douglas has over twenty years of experience in safeguarding, including a variety of roles, such as Senior Social Worker, Assistant Team Manager, Team Manager, Policy and Quality Assurance Manager, and she is currently the Professional Lead for Social Work at the University of Hertfordshire.

Julie Fourie has well over a decade of experience in safeguarding vulnerable children as Senior Social Worker, Team Manager and now Family Court Advisor/Children's Guardian.

Together, they have a real passion for social work and safeguarding, and equipping others to do this job well.

Foreword from the Series Editor

This book is written by two professionals who have extensive experience of safeguarding children, young people and families. I am delighted that we have this text in the Post Qualifying Social Work series as this is such an important area of professional practice, one that practitioners in this field face every day of their working lives.

There are numerous textbooks on safeguarding, but what sets this book apart is the 'how to' element. The tools that Vida Douglas and Julie Fourie have developed are easy to use and break down safeguarding assessment and decision-making. The book is full of case examples that professionals are likely to come across, allowing social workers and professionals with safeguarding responsibilities to apply their knowledge to a case situation. It is a much-needed text to support social workers and other professionals in meeting their safeguarding responsibilities.

This book embeds equality and diversity throughout, reflects on the implications of remote ways of working in a COVID-19 era and encourages you to think and apply safeguarding knowledge. The book supports professionals involved in safeguarding to make a professional judgement about assessing and managing risk in safeguarding children, young people and their families.

To those of you working in this complex field of safeguarding children, young people and families can I not only commend this text to you but also sincerely thank you for all your hard work and dedication in making our society both a safer and better place to live. The social work profession is often misunderstood and, frankly, rarely appreciated by society as a whole, yet it makes a massive difference to individuals, families and communities. This text is part of a wider series of textbooks designed to support and encourage the best possible professional practice – I am honoured to be the series editor and to work with simply wonderful people who want to share their knowledge and expertise. Together may we never give up the call to make a difference within our society.

Professor Keith Brown
Founding Director of The National Centre for Post-Qualifying Social Work and Professional Practice (NCPQSWPP)

Centre for Leadership, Impact and Management Bournemouth (CLiMB)

Introduction

The inspiration for this book has come from our love for the profession of social work and the real differences we know that it has made to the lives of children and their families we have personally worked with over the years. This book is in honour of the children we have had the privilege to meet, sometimes in extremely difficult circumstances, and seeks to represent their voices about what they have said they need from social workers who assess and make plans to support them to feel safe, and able to live a happy and fulfilled life. We are acutely aware that to keep children safe and well requires their parents, carers and the professionals who have contact with children (e.g. teachers, nursery staff, health visitors and nurses) to work together and actively play their part in safeguarding. Safeguarding is everyone's responsibility.

We have been fortunate to work with students embarking on a course to be social workers and those who are newly qualified social workers, and in our experiences have identified there is a gap to bridge: how do we actually safeguard children and young people? There is a gap in the current practical resources available. The influence and impact all professionals have on the lives of children, young people and families is deep and far-reaching, and we need to get this right. We envisage that this book will be a much needed and necessary hands-on guide in supporting social workers, and professionals with safeguarding responsibilities, in how to carry out their safeguarding roles effectively and which allows safe outcomes for children and young people.

The COVID-19 pandemic has impacted on how training is delivered, and how we do social work. We need to ensure that in our new remote ways of learning and working, we continue to put the child at the centre of our decision-making. This is something our book addresses.

This book will guide social work students, newly qualified social workers as well as experienced social workers in their direct practice and intervention with children and families.

We have developed a range of toolkits that will support you in thinking about risk in very practical terms. The focus of this book will give insight into the assessment, interventions and the skills required to effectively and confidently make things better and safer in the lives of vulnerable children. This book will do the following:

- Develop good practice: through providing case examples and question to promote reflection and self-learning

- Provide took kits: a framework of prompts and practical solutions to develop skills, knowledge and behaviours in assessment and intervention with children and families

- Apply law and social policy in everyday practice.

Overview of chapters

The book consists of eight chapters, and we have developed a tool to explain safeguarding and promote safeguarding decision-making. Each chapter develops the features of this tool, and considers the key issues influencing safeguarding, including equality and diversity and remote ways of working in a COVID-19 era. There is also a feature in each chapter to promote your own professional development journey offering you space to think about and apply your developing safeguarding knowledge.

Chapter 1: Safeguarding: setting the scene

This chapter introduces the concept of safeguarding and recognises the role of parents, families, carers, social workers and other professionals in this complex task. Safeguarding children and young people is a responsibility for everyone. In this chapter, we introduce you to our Safeguarding Assessment and Decision-Making Tool, and the key concepts of safeguarding which are: identifying and measuring risk and protective factors, making judgements on the level of risk the child is exposed to and providing interventions to make things better for the child and young person. A selection of case studies is provided so that you can begin to explore this key concept and our Safeguarding Assessment and Decision-making tool.

Chapter 2: The voice of the child and young person

Safeguarding starts with hearing the voice of the child. It is about gaining insight into the child or young person's perception and understanding of how they view what life is like for them. Communication with children must be child-focused and the content of what is spoken about with the child must be age-appropriate and in line with their development and understanding, and any additional needs they have. The chapter outlines the five principles of effective communication and summarises the three stages of good communication with children. The chapter provides you with strategies and communication tools to emphatically engage with children and young people, both in person and remotely, to hear about their lived experiences. COVID-19 means we are integrating remote ways of working into safeguarding practice, and this chapter sets out guidance on when to proceed with an in-person visit or remote visit when undertaking direct work with children, young people and their families.

Chapter 3: Communicating with adults and professionals

Communication with adults, including carers of children and professionals, is a key part of safeguarding. The focus of communication with adults is different to communication with children. With adults, we must challenge a parent's style or way of parenting which is causing harm to a child; or we must challenge a professional when there is a difference of opinion about what is in a child's best interest. The chapter provides practice tips on how to communicate with adults to motivate them to change and take up their safeguarding responsibilities, drawing on our practice experience, The Cycle of Change model (Prochaska and Di Clemente, 1982), and principles of motivational interviewing.

Chapter 4: Assessment: managing risk and decision-making

This chapter hones in on safeguarding and sets out how to assess a child's or young person's circumstances, manage risk and make safe decisions for them. The key tasks of assessment are gathering information, assessing the information gathered and making recommendations. These concepts are explained using our Safeguarding Assessment and Decision-Making Tool. The complexity of safeguarding lies in the analysis of the information gathered. How do we weigh up the risk of harm in the information gathered to determine safety for a child? In this chapter, we share some assessment tools, and introduce you to our Risk Analysis and Management Tool which supports your thinking of risk and helps you to break down and understand risk in a practical way to make professional judgements of whether a child or young person is suffering significant harm. Assessments are formally recorded as a written document, a report, and principles of good reports, such as evidence-based and defensible decision-making, are discussed.

Chapter 5: Interventions: achieving good outcomes

What happens after the assessment stage matters most to children and young people. To make things better for them, social workers must formulate a child-focused intervention plan and identify relevant change work to address the assessed risk. We need to motivate children, young people, parents and professionals to engage in interventions. Importantly, we must monitor the progress, assess change and make evidence-based decisions on whether interventions should end, alternative support must be provided or the case escalated due to increasing safeguarding concerns. This chapter provides reflective exercises to practice formulating effective intervention plans.

Chapter 6: Court work

Going to court is a last resort, but social workers need to be prepared and knowledgeable about the court process. In this chapter, the social worker's role and responsibilities in court work are identified using a case study to explain the stages of the court process. A key intervention in court work is contact—the time the child and young person should spend with their family. Local authorities have duties to promote family relationships when safe to do so. Making contact recommendations is complex, and we have devised, and introduced you to, our Contact Recommendations Tool to help you assess the risks of contact and formulate safe contact recommendations.

Chapter 7: Resilience in safeguarding children, young people and families

Safeguarding children, young people and families can be emotionally challenging as we come across hurt and suffering. Resilience is needed. Maintaining personal and professional well-being is imperative if we are to make safe and informed decisions for children and young people. The chapter provides strategies that can support professionals working across a range of sectors with responsibilities in safeguarding to be resilient, including our Well-being Index Tool, which sets out six key factors important to well-being and resilience that should be discussed in supervision.

Chapter 8: Checklists for effective practice

The book ends with a checklist for effective practice by looking at the key responsibilities of a social worker and actions to be taken when safeguarding children, young people and families under the different frameworks, including Child in Need (CIN), Child Protection (CP), Public Law Outline and Care Proceedings and Children Looked After (CLA).

Concluding comments

Professionals working with vulnerable children need to make professional judgements on whether a child has suffered or is at risk of suffering significant harm, and the tools we have developed in this book will support you in this important role.

Chapter 1
Safeguarding: setting the scene

Chapter objectives

This chapter seeks to answer these questions:

- What is safeguarding?

- How to assess risk and safeguard children and young people?

- What is risk?

- Who is responsible for safeguarding?

- Why is safeguarding important?

- What are the legal frameworks around safeguarding?

Introduction

If you are reading this book, you are interested in understanding safeguarding. Safeguarding is concerned with ensuring a person is free from harm, risk and danger; and that the individual can access the support they need to thrive and do well in life.

The culture of most societies is to look after those who are young, old and vulnerable. For example, in the United Kingdom during World War II, children were evacuated out of cities to protect them from the dangers of war. There is an innate duty of care and regard for one another which is a part of human nature. This is further demonstrated in the United Kingdom, where like many countries, it has an ageing population, and to support this group there are a range of services such as meals on wheels, telecare equipment and home care agencies to promote independent or semi-independent living in the community. Perhaps this aspect of human nature is most vividly seen during the COVID-19 pandemic, where many retired NHS staff and community volunteers put themselves forward to help care for those critically ill and otherwise affected by the virus. There has been a surge of online support groups to promote individual physical and mental well-being whilst people are encouraged to self-isolate, and companies have made available a range of education resources to support home learning for children and young people during national lockdowns.

At a national level, the government is interested in the well-being of children and young people. The Department of Education carries out yearly analysis on children in care and produces child protection/in need statistics to deliberate whether as a nation we are meeting the needs of our vulnerable children and young people, and providing them with the opportunities to achieve, thrive and reach their potential. How well we safeguard our most vulnerable matters too. In the United Kingdom, Ofsted is commissioned as an inspection and regulatory organisation which reviews and monitors the services that local authorities, education provisions and childcare homes provide, pushing them to meet statutory care requirements and to continually raise the standard of care. A report is produced following the inspection to help drive improvements and make individuals and organisations accountable for safeguarding practices and arrangements.

Individuals, families, local community organisations, universal services and local and national government all have a vested interest in promoting the safety and wellbeing of the most vulnerable. When it comes to safeguarding children, this becomes a responsibility for everyone. To understand this, it is helpful to use the image of an onion. The child or young person is always at the centre, and individuals, families, universal services and local and national government form layers of protection around the child. The responsibility of safeguarding starts with parents or carers and stretches across to the highest authorities. We know only too well the consequences of failing to safeguard, which is documented in numerous serious case reviews and enquiries into child deaths in the United Kingdom. Effective safeguarding practice is a must and requires professionals, agencies and individuals and families to work together to provide the right environment and opportunities for our most vulnerable children to be safe, well and fulfilled.

We are passionate about safeguarding and getting things right for children and young people. Safeguarding is a complex task, and, in this book, we hope to make it tangible for you. We will bring the concepts of safeguarding practice to life, equipping you with the how-to skills to be effective in your safeguarding role. We will develop your understanding and application of safeguarding practice through case studies and reflective questions, as well as considering key issues influencing safeguarding, including equality and diversity and remote ways of working in a COVID-19 era. We will promote your own professional development journey, offering you space to think about and apply your developing safeguarding knowledge.

To safeguard effectively, we first need to understand what safeguarding is, why we do it and the law around it. Therefore, this chapter sets the scene for safeguarding.

What is safeguarding?

Safeguarding is the verb given to the interventions required to keep a child or young person safe from harm and promote their well-being. How we do this is both influenced by the values society holds around what is acceptable, or what is considered harm or danger, and is shaped by our reflective social work practice over time. There has been an emphasis on *child protection*, and interventions being focused on actively protecting children and young people from harm. This is seen in the statistics published by the Department of Education in the report *Children Looked after in England (including Adoption) year ending 31.03.2019 (2019)*, which shows a steady rise in the number of care proceedings cases over the last ten years. Isabelle Trowler (Chief Social Worker for England) has analysed this in a research report and puts forward a case for 'clear blue water': the notion that there should be a clear distinction between families where under no circumstances can a child or young person be kept safe at home, and families where there is identified risk of significant harm, but there is the possibility of this risk being managed through other innovative interventions (Trowler, 2018). The statistics on the outcomes for children in care show that they have below average outcomes across a range of measures, although children in care make better progress in some areas than children in need, a closer comparison group (NSPCC, January 2020). The Children in Care statistics and research on the outcomes for children are shaping social work intervention, and social work interventions are now focusing on *safeguarding*, active interventions to keep the child safe. Whilst the terms child protection and safeguarding are often used interchangeably, the distinguishing feature of the shift towards safeguarding is the concept of *managing risk*.

How to assess risk and safeguard children and young people?

The following section will introduce you to two key concepts in safeguarding children and young people: assessment and risk.

Assessing risk in practice

The crux of safeguarding and assessing harm is identifying the risk and protective factors in the child's life. To do this, you must first gather information about the concern raised. You must speak to the child or young person to ascertain how life is like for them. You will need to speak to the parents, both mother and father (or a significant carer), to ascertain their understanding and insight into the concern, their willingness to engage and work with professionals to make things better and their motivation to change. You must also speak to other professionals to get information about the child's health and development needs, the parenting they receive and the wider environmental supports available. After you have gathered information, you must assess risk. From the information gathered, you need to weigh up what are the risk, vulnerability and protective factors you have identified. Risk and vulnerability factors are the 'bad' experiences in a child's life that are causing harm or increasing the likelihood of harm. Protective factors are the experiences and strengths in a child's life that mitigate or reduce risk. You must assess the impact of these factors and consider what they mean for the child's safety and well-being. You will need to make professional judgements and determine if the child is at risk of suffering significant harm or is suffering significant harm, and you must consider whether the risk can be managed. Finally, you must come up with an intervention plan, which focuses on ensuring the professionals and the family work collaboratively to keep the child or young person safe and improve their outcomes.

Assessment and decision-making tool

We have developed a tool to explain safeguarding and promote safeguarding decision-making. The model draws on ideas from DOH Assessment Framework, Calder (2008) Risk and Resilience Model, and the legal frameworks which underpin safeguarding practice. The key elements of the tool form the basis of the chapters for this book.

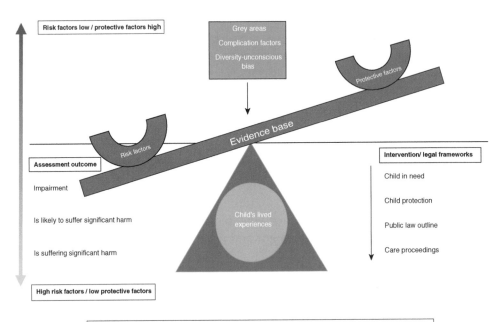

Safeguarding decision-making tool

The tool depicts a balance scale. The base of the scale is the DOH Assessment Framework, encouraging a practitioner to gather information about the child's lived experiences, including their individual needs, the parenting they receive and the environment they live in. The scale balance is the evidence base for safeguarding practice and requires analytic thinking. It requires a practitioner to consider the following:

- What do I know about the child's circumstances?

- How do I know this? For example, is this something a child or parent has told me, a professional observation or a report from another professional?

- What are the complicating factors? For example, are there gaps in information? What are the culture and diversity issues? Is there unconscious bias? Are any of your underlying personal and professional attitudes, beliefs and experiences impacting on your understanding and assessment of risk? How can this be mitigated?

- What does this mean for the child? Is it causing them harm or placing them at risk of suffering harm; or is it a protective factor?

The identified risk and protective factors are separated and balanced out. The higher the number of risks and lower the number of protective factors, the more likely higher level of statutory intervention is required. The assessment of the level of risk the child is exposed to, for example, impairment, likely to suffer significant harm, is suffering significant harm, must be considered against the level of statutory intervention required, such as involvement under Child in Need, Child Protection, Public Law Outline and Care Proceedings, respectively.

Test out your safeguarding knowledge and risk assessment by using our Safeguarding Assessment and Decision-making tool to make an assessment on the following case study.

CASE STUDY

The Local Authority receives a safeguarding referral from Children's A&E department. A mother has presented with her baby to Children's A&E and disclosed that she held her baby by her neck this morning in frustration, which has left bruising around the baby's neck. The mother is reported to be very tearful and remorseful. She was at home on her own when the incident took place.

Reflective questions

What are the risk and protective factors?

What legal framework would you assess under?

What other factors could increase or lower risk?

Comment

What risks and protective factors did you identify? In this case study marks have been left on the baby and the baby has sustained a non-accidental injury, which is a safeguarding concern. It is a strength that the mother has immediately accessed support and not tried to hide the incident, and that she is remorseful, accepting the harm she has caused. Professional judgement as to which framework to manage the case under will be impacted by the further information you gather.

For example, is there another protective adult such as the father or any other family member who can provide support? Is the mother willing to engage with support services? What were the circumstances leading up to this incident? On the basis of the limited information in this case study, the case could be managed under Child In Need. However, if, for example, the bruising was found by chance from an observation made by a health visitor at a standard appointment, and the mother was disengaging, the risk would increase, suggesting the need for a higher framework of intervention, such as child protection is required.

This case study shows the importance of assessing risks and strengths in safeguarding and managing risk.

What is risk?

The concept of risk is central to safeguarding. Risk is an action or behaviour considered harmful to a child or young person, and may be detrimental to his or her safety and well-being. There are four categories of risk in safeguarding: physical harm, sexual harm, emotional harm and neglect. Whilst these are four separate categories of risk, often the impact of the harm experienced by the child or young person spreads across one or more of the four categories. The categories of harm are often interlinked. For example, a child who experiences sexual harm through child sexual exploitation may also be experiencing, or at risk of experiencing, physical harm where physical force may be used to get a child to perform a sexual activity, and may also experience emotional harm through these experiences. Similarly, a child who witnesses domestic abuse will be at risk of emotional and physical harm through being either intentionally or unintentionally caught up in the crossfire of physical altercations.

The understanding of harm or risk is linked to the values society holds at a moment in time. For example, in the United Kingdom, during the 1700–1800s it was socially acceptable for children to be married in their teenage years, whereas now this can be viewed as a safeguarding concern. Therefore, when assessing the risk of harm it is important to understand the social context of each society and the impact of the behaviour: what does this mean for the child or young person? Will it cause harm? Is the harm caused significant? As a professional in the care sector, it is possible you will come across a teenage marriage scenario. (In England, the minimum legal age to enter into a marriage is 16 years, although this requires parental consent.) It will be important to understand from the young person what their wishes are about a teenage marriage; and what will the impact be. If it is against their wishes and will stop them achieving their aspirations, this could be considered harmful. However, if it is their wish and they will continue to have the same opportunities, this would lower the risk.

We will now look at a further case study.

COVID-19 is on the rise and the government is asking all citizens to stay at home to keep themselves safe and prevent the virus from spreading. During a video call you find out a family has not been following national guidelines on social distancing. The mother took her child to A&E as he was feeling unwell. The hospital wanted to complete a COVID-19 test, but the mother self-discharged the child against medical advice.

Reflective question

Is this a safeguarding concern? Why? Why not?

Comment

Failure to follow guidelines is not necessarily a safeguarding concern. However, it's the parental responses to the child that need assessing, such as exposing the child to health risks and then not following through on health advice or seeking appropriate treatment. In assessing risk, you will need to consider whether the child's health needs are being met and promoted, and whether this is an isolated incident or pattern of behaviour.

If the government implemented more stringent rules and passed COVID-19 social distancing laws, society would perceive this risk differently and it would likely be seen as a safeguarding risk factor requiring statutory intervention.

Culture, diversity, religion and risk

We live in a diverse society and people have different experiences of parenting as well as cultural views and norms about what risk or harm is. To continue the example, the practice of arranged (forced) marriages within some cultures is considered culturally acceptable. This is not promoted in the United Kingdom and is illegal (Anti-Social Behaviour, Crime and Policing Act 2014). Therefore, when considering safeguarding concerns it is important to understand where the behaviour comes from, promote child-focused discussions on the impact of the behaviour on the child, share new ways of doing and promote awareness of what the law stipulates to be acceptable behaviour. In the case of arranged (forced) marriages, this is breaking the law, and escalates safeguarding concerns.

We will now look at safeguarding and issues of culture, religion and risk in the case study below.

A 12-year-old child requires surgery for a health need. The family are Jehovah Witnesses and refusing to give consent for the surgery as it is against their religious beliefs. A referral is made from the hospital who are worried the child's health is being harmed.

Reflective questions

How much weight must be given to cultural and religious beliefs in assessing harm?

What factors must be considered and balanced in identifying risk to the child and ensuring their safety?

Comment

Safeguarding and identifying risk is complex. In your approach to understanding and assessing risk it is important to closely examine the child's circumstances with a pointed focus on what the evidence is and what this means for the child's right to be healthy, safe and thrive. This must be balanced against whether the intervention and disruption to a family's right to private life is proportionate and necessary. Issues to consider in making a safeguarding assessment in this case study include the following:

- What is the impact on the child of not having medical intervention? Will it lead to death or significant health implications impacting on the child's daily life, or is the impact minimal?

- Does the child want the medical treatment? Is the child Gillick competent? Gillick competence is a term used to consider whether a child is mature enough to make their own decision about things that affect them, like whether they want/consent to a surgery (NSPCC, June 2020).

Parental insight and assessing risk

With an ever-increasing focus on making things safe for the child or young person, a key factor to assess in safeguarding assessments is parental insight into the concerns and motivation to change. Without this, change is unlikely and not sustainable. This is a key element of the Family Safeguarding Model (2017) developed by Hertfordshire County Council, which is now been shared and practiced in other local authorities. The Family Safeguarding Model was developed following analysis of key performance indicators which showed children had been on child protection plans for long periods of time with no shift in the safeguarding concerns. It is an innovative reform to children's services which uses motivational interviewing to improve outcomes for children. The pilot showed the reform was impactful, with a reduction in the number of cases allocated, and a reduction in use of child protection (CP) plans as key service outcomes. This is set out in Family Safeguarding Hertfordshire Evaluation Report, July 2017.

To effectively safeguard, we need to support and enable parents to be child focused and make use of their social and professional networks. That's when safety becomes manageable. However, there are times when risk cannot be managed, and a child or young person is not safe, and therefore statutory guidance and processes must be initiated and followed, for example, S47 of the Children Act 1989 duty to investigate cases of risk or S31 of the Children Act 1989 to consider threshold for court orders (www.legislation.gov.uk).

REFLECTION QUESTION

Reflect on the above case examples, the family failing to follow COVID-19 guidelines and the family refusing surgery for their child for religious reasons.

How can you motivate a parent to change?

Comment

What are your ideas? Compare them to the practice tips and examples in motivating change which are discussed in Chapter 3.

Who is responsible for safeguarding?

Parents and caregivers are held responsible for protecting and safeguarding vulnerable children and young people. However, due to the failure of parents and caregivers over the years to adequately safeguard their child, this responsibility should not only rest with parents/caregivers alone. If a society is to protect and safeguard its children, then the responsibility should be shared. According to *Working Together to Safeguard Children* (2018), a statutory guidance on inter-agency working, the responsibility for safeguarding lies with everyone. It states that:

> *Everyone who works with children has a responsibility for keeping them safe. No single practitioner can have a full picture of a child's needs and circumstances and, if children and families are to receive the right help at the right time, everyone who comes into contact with them has a role to play in identifying concerns, sharing information and taking prompt action.*

> *(2018: 10)*

To ensure that safeguarding is actively undertaken, certain professions have been given a legal duty to lead safeguarding in their organisations. These individuals are referred to as 'designated safeguarding leads' and they offer guidance when there are concerns about a child's welfare in the organisation, identifying and agreeing the actions to be taken and ensuring that all actions are recorded. Central to the work of the designated lead is ensuring that all those involved in supporting and caring for the young person in their organisation are adequately trained to safeguard.

As individuals and citizens of a community we all are responsible for being curious, vigilant and aware enough to see when a child or young person is at risk or in need of support and intervention to alleviate the risk and suffering, they are or likely to experience.

The following case study looks at the concept of shared responsibility in safeguarding children and young people.

CASE STUDY

You are a duty social worker and receive a call from a concerned member of the community saying that she often hears her neighbours arguing and the children crying.

Reflective questions

Think about the above case. How would you respond to the above information?

It could be that the information is malicious hearsay. However, we should always respond to concerns of risk to children. The Local Authority (LA) where the child lives will need to make enquiries to be satisfied if any action is required to safeguard and promote the welfare of the child. The enquiry will be completed by a social worker, undertaking relevant checks with agencies, such as schools and the general practitioner to find out what is already known about the child and their family. The social worker will visit the child at home and talk to them about the concerns raised. During the home visit the social worker will establish whether the best interest of the child is being met and identify any support required to promote the child's welfare and well-being.

Why is safeguarding important?

The Office for National Statistics (ONS) in their recent 2019 publication, 'Child abuse in England and Wales' reported that one in five adults in England and Wales had experienced abuse under the age of sixteen. Furthermore, over 8.5 million people aged between 18 and 74 have either experienced or witnessed abuse. The extent of abuse is wide, and the human costs are chronic and enduring, resulting in many living the effects of abuse in terms of their emotional and mental well-being.

Child abuse enquiries and deaths are a tragic consequence of a failure to safeguard and is perhaps the most poignant and forceful reason for why safeguarding matters. If we are to truly change the outcomes of children, then safeguarding must matter. Fostering a climate that encourages questions about current practices and strategies that educate caregivers about the impact of inadequate safeguarding is why safeguarding should always be on the agenda and matter to us all.

What are the legal frameworks around safeguarding?

In England, safeguarding is informed by the legal framework of the Children Act 1989. This legislation sets out key principles to guide agencies determining risk and when to intervene. Underpinning this legislation are several principles. A key principle is centred around the importance of the welfare of the child. Securing and protecting the welfare of a child should be uppermost when guiding our actions and interventions. The act also promotes the responsibility of parents in safeguarding by defining what parental responsibility is, who has parental responsibility and in what circumstances parental responsibility can be shared with other agencies. Where possible, parents should retain parental responsibilities and agencies must work in partnership with parents. Agencies' duty to protect and intervene is enshrined within section 47 of the 1989 Children Act:

> (b) the authority shall make, or cause to be made, such inquiries as they consider necessary to enable them to decide whether they should take any actions to safeguard or promote the child's welfare.
>
> (Children Act 1989, S47)

Local authorities delegate this responsibility to social workers who are required to ascertain the level of risk a child or young person may be or has experienced and then determine whether the risks will result in harm and impact significantly on their well-being. A more detailed explanation of the legislative framework will be explored in future chapters.

Social work: a reflective and evolving profession

In your practice as a social worker, you are asked to stop and think about what you did, how you did it, did your approach achieve a good outcome, what is the learning, could something have been done better and how you might implement new behaviours. This is called 'reflective practice'. The model of reflective practice stems from Schon (1983). The social work profession and how we safeguard children and young people has been shaped by such reflections and learning. The findings from the enquiries into the death of Victoria Climbe and Baby P (Peter Connolly) are perhaps the most well-known and pivotal cases that have influenced safeguarding practice in England. Lord Laming's 2003 report, *The Victoria Climbie*

Inquiry, brought changes to child protection legislation including the production of The Children Act (2004) and Working Together (2004). Lord Laming's second report, *The protection of children in England: a progress* report (2009), made 58 recommendations for child protection reform. Professor Eileen Munro was commissioned to review social work and, in her report *A child centred system* (2011), she made recommendations for more child-focused interventions and increasing the scope of analytical thinking and professional judgement in decision-making to work more purposefully with families. Josh McAllister has recently been commissioned to undertake a further independent review of children's social care. As you can see from the outcome of these reports, reflection is important and necessary to safeguarding children and young people effectively. We also therefore have a professional duty to keep our knowledge of safeguarding practice up to date.

Diversity and equality in safeguarding

Effective safeguarding requires the social work practitioner to reflect on their practice and to consider how our involvement with children and their families promotes diversity and equality in the safeguarding process. To support your reflection in this area we have included an equality and diversity section, with a series of questions for you to consider in each chapter.

REFLECTIVE QUESTIONS

Consider how you can demonstrate respect and value for the families culture/religion. For example, what you can do before a meeting?	Ask yourself what information would help you understand the equality and diversity need of the family.	Check out your understanding of the diversity and equality needs of the child and their family.	Is there any bias in the information collected/ obtained?

Safeguarding and a remote way of working

Social work is a reflective and evolving profession. We need to reflect not only on our direct practice and how to improve this but also the changing social context in which we safeguard children and young people. COVID-19, the global health pandemic, has forced the world into a remote way of working and has significantly impacted on how we approach safeguarding children and families. For example, face-to-face visits, which used to be the norm, now only happen on an essential basis. Interventions, like parenting courses or domestic abuse work, take place on video platforms. Whilst this is starting to look different and there are more technological-based interactions and interventions being used, this does not change our safeguarding responsibility or what the key elements of safeguarding are. As we unpack how to safeguard in this book, we will discuss and reflect upon the issues of remote working in safeguarding children and young people as key feature in each chapter.

REFLECTIVE QUESTIONS

How has remote working impacted on your safeguarding practice?

How can you prepare and support children and their families to engage with remote working?

How has remote working impacted on your resilience and well-being?

Chapter summary

- Safeguarding is to ensure a child or young person is safe, happy and has better day-to-day experiences. Whilst this is put simply, achieving this is often a complex task.

- Whilst there's a natural disposition for individuals, communities, organisations and governments to care for others and keep them safe, there are also legal mandates which cut across these sectors that state safeguarding is everybody's responsibility.

The key elements of safeguarding are as follows:

- *Identifying risk and protective factors*: Having an evidence base for the concerns and strengths. What are they and where do they come from?

- *Measuring risk*: understanding the impact of these factors on the safety and well-being of the child. What do they mean for the child?

- Consider parental insight into concerns and motivation to change

- *Making judgements*: is the child suffering or at risk of suffering significant harm? Can the risk be managed?

- *Intervention*: come up with a care plan on how to keep the child safe and make things better.

YOUR LEARNING JOURNEY

In this book we want to demystify safeguarding and equip you with the practical skills to do this well and so make things safe for children and young people. As you work through this book, we would encourage you to stop and think about how you can apply your learning in your day-to-day safeguarding practice. We will give you space to record your learning journey at the end of each chapter.

Below are a few questions for you to consider about safeguarding.

- Before reading this chapter, how much did you know about safeguarding?

- Are there gaps in your knowledge?

- How can you develop your safeguarding knowledge and practice?

Chapter 2
The voice of the child and young person

Chapter objectives

This chapter seeks to answer these questions:

- What is communication?

- Why do we need to communicate with children and young people?

- What do we mean by child-focused communication?

- What is good communication?

- What are effective communication tools?

Introduction

Happy, healthy and safe children is the primary goal of most parents, and all adults working with children and young people. Children and families social workers are regularly involved in safeguarding matters, where children and young people are the focus of this work. We are required to make decisions about their lives that are impactful and long-lasting. Since you will be making decisions about children and young people, it is only right that you hear their voice about what their day-to-day experiences are like, and what they want to happen.

As summarised in the Working Together to Safeguard Children (2018) report:

> Anyone working with children should see and speak to the child: listen to what they say, take their views seriously, and work with them and their families collaboratively when deciding how to support their need.
>
> (Working Together to Safeguard Children, 2018: 10)

Listening to the voice of the child and responding to their requests will ensure that they are kept at the heart of our decision-making. In order to fulfil these responsibilities, as a social worker or health-care professional we need to be able to communicate effectively.

This chapter looks at communication, and how we can engage with children and young people to understand what life is like for them and include their wishes and feelings in the assessments we do and the safeguarding decisions we make.

What is communication?

Theories of child development (such as Jean Piaget, Lev Vygotsky, Mary Ainsworth, Albert Bandura) have emphasised the importance of the formative years in the development of children. Children develop emotional, social, behavioural, cognitive and communication skills which are the foundation for adult life. We will turn our attention to why it is important to communicate with children and young people. However, first it is important to define what we understand by the term communication.

Communication is the act of sharing an idea, opinion or emotion. Communication requires a receiver and giver of the message. Communication can be both verbal and non-verbal, but equally powerful in transmitting a thought or view. For example, if you attend a home visit and the young person refuses to talk with you, they are communicating a powerful message. Communication can be problematic because the message can be misunderstood by the receiver due to differing perspectives, experiences, values and cultural beliefs that influences how we interpret the communicated message.

Despite the potential for miscommunication, health and social care professionals need to communicate with children and young people. Communication is powerful because it can educate, encourage, promote a sense of belonging and offer comfort and hope in challenging and unsure periods of a child's life (for example, the death of a loved one).

Why do we need to communicate with children and young people?

For the health or social work professional working with children and young people, the aim of our involvement should be to make things safe and better for children. This requires those working with children to get to know the child. As we get to know the child and begin to build a relationship, our primary aim is to hear the voice of the child. To do this, we must understand the following:

- What is important to the child?
- How does the situation make them feel?
- And more importantly, how do they want you to help?

We must be deliberate in our actions to put aside our own voice as we begin to learn the voice of the child. This requires us to value and respect the messages communicated by children even if it is not fully understood. Our role is to develop an awareness of what is important to the child and together make sense of the message being communicated.

We have a legal mandate under the Children Act 1989 to ensure that in our interventions and decision-making the welfare of the child is paramount. To inform our decisions we must gain the views and wishes of the children we work with, and where possible advocate their wishes. However, there are instances when the voice of the child cannot be at the forefront of our decision-making if it means that the child or young person is unable to identify or protect themselves from risk. In those situations, the reasons why we do not support the children's wishes and feelings must be explained.

Our communications with children and young people have the potential to affect a child or young person and leave an indelible footprint in their lives. For instance, if we arrange to meet a young person and we turn up late, or worse still, cancel the appointment, the take-home message for the young person might be that they are not a priority. Our communication does matter, and we need to get it right.

The voice of the child is important when completing our assessments as it tells the young person that their feelings, views and hopes for the future matter. Our assessments are an influential communication tool for the voice of the child. Their voice should be fairly and appropriately recorded, and it is important that they are also given the opportunity to confirm that the assessment is a true and valid representation of their voice.

As we communicate with children and young people, we should be guided by five principles:

- *Child centred*
  - You understand the child's lived experiences and the support they need to make them safe
- *Context specific*
  - The environment we communicate with children can be formal or informal. The child's environment will shape and influence what and when they choose to communicate and how confidently they communicate.
- *Encouragement*
  - Using a strength-based approach our communication should be positive, recognising the child's strengths.
- *Value their experiences*
  - Listen and understand the child's voice. We should always represent the views of the child honestly and fairly.
- *Promote discovery*
  - As we communicate, we should encourage children and young people to be curious and ask questions. Make time for periods of discovery in our communications with young people.

- *How can you use these principles in your communication with children and your people?*

These principles highlight that our communication with children and young people is not just about extracting information but also about building relationships and exploring with children their role in making sure they are happy, healthy and safe.

Chapter 3 discusses the concept of challenge in communication, the notion of supporting people to do things differently. This is pertinent in our communication with children and young people, as there will be times when we will need to challenge children and *promote their discovery* of why they are doing things in a certain way, for example, displaying challenging behaviours such as going missing regularly or aggressive behaviours. Let's consider this in the following case study.

CASE STUDY

A child aged thirteen years old is removed from her mother's care following the conclusion of a contested hearing. At age thirteen years she has developed a strong attachment to her mother, albeit a harmful and enmeshed attachment. The courts have considered the matter and made a judgement that the lesser harm is for her to be removed from her mother's care. This young girl struggles emotionally with this decision. She is placed in a residential unit, the placement identified to best meet her needs, and displays aggressive and threatening behaviours towards care staff. Whilst this behaviour is understood and emotional support is being provided, her continued behaviour means she has intentionally harmed staff, and the placement breaks down. She needs to move to a new placement. The young girl likes her new placement, she has a big room, has formed a relationship with her key worker and has access to activities she enjoys. After a settling in period, her threatening and aggressive behaviours re-start. Whilst it is acknowledged that this young girl feels hurt and is angry and misses her mother, she also needs to understand that it is a permanent decision, and that if her purposeful threatening and aggressive behaviour towards care staff continues, she is at risk of moving placement again and rupturing the relationships she is building. She needs to be challenged about this.

Comment

We should always seek to understand behaviour; behaviour is a form of communication. It is necessary to use appropriate forms of communication to help the child or young person think about what is a good choice and what is a bad choice, and what is the impact or consequences of making those choices.

What do we mean by child-focused communication?

Child-focused communication is communicating using words that the child or young person can understand, and ensuring that the content of what is spoken about is age-appropriate. This means that what we share with the child or young person must be proportionate to their cognitive and emotional development and understanding. To better understand these two aspects of child-focused communication, let us think about the issue of domestic abuse. If you say to a 5-year-old child, 'the professionals think there is domestic abuse between your mother and father', the child is unlikely to understand what you are talking about. The words 'professional' and 'domestic abuse' are big words that are content laden and likely outside of the child's vocabulary at this age. It is better to say something like, 'the grownups are worried that mummy and daddy fight and sometimes hurt each other'. This is the language that a child can understand and relate to. You then need to make judgements about how much of the issues of domestic abuse should be shared with the child. This will depend on how perceptive the child is about their lived experiences and what they in turn communicate back to you. Through your communication their behaviour and reactions will help you to determine their level of distress and whether they are ready to hear any more. Think about delivering important messages, in small doses. Give some information to the child and leave them to think about what you have said. Just like adults hearing a difficult message, it may take time for them to process and make sense of it. It might be that on your second visit you can open up and develop the conversation. What is shared should not cause the child unnecessary worry. Often it is appropriate for the child to know the headline issues, and not necessarily the details of these.

The following activity will support you to develop your practice skills in child-focused communication.

---

*ACTIVITY **2.1***

The following words are key phrases used in safeguarding children and young people. How would you frame them or explain them to use in your discussions with a child or young person?

- *Assessment*
- *Child protection conference*
- *Happy and safe*

Comment

Take the example of the words 'happy and safe'. We know children can express feelings through their smiles, laughter and behaviour. You might encourage them to think about a recent event, such a birthday or the arrival of a new pet or sibling, to explore their understanding of 'happy', and then get them to think about in what other environments, such as at home or school, they experience similar feelings. Do not forget to use props, for example, interactive tools such as crafts and toys.

You will see from this activity that it can be hard to simplify phrases when they are intrinsic to us. However, if we are to engage effectively with children and young people, they must be able to make sense of what we are saying to them. The language we choose is important. When engaging with children and young people, it is important that we are mindful of a child's age, developmental stage and any additional needs to ensure communication is pitched in a way the child or young person can understand and respond to.

Table 2.1 shows the key things to consider about children when communicating across the different age groups.

Now that we have looked at what child-focused communication entails, we are going to explore how you can apply this in practice through the following case study examples.

Table 2.1   Developmental stages and child-focused communication

0–5 years	5–13 years	13–16 years	16–18 years
To seek attention/ assistance from the caregiver (cry). This creates a sense of security and belonging. Awareness of emotions (worry if a caregiver leaves the room or someone new enters the room) Learn new experiences and develop new skills (learning to count) Build relationships, play and interact with others through simple sentences and touch (pulling at their caregiver by the hand to get their attention)	Language is used to test out and investigate their surroundings Show their emotions through words, behaviour (express excitement with food!) Beginning to understand feelings and emotions of others (friends in school) To experiment and draw on the experiences of key others to solve/ understand a problem/situation (teacher)	Develop friendships to build their confidence and positive sense of self. Explore situations which might present them with risks to understand their own wishes and begin to take protective steps with the guidance from an adult To develop new friendships and be allowed to make mistakes and seek guidance from a positive role model.	Communication skills become highly developed and are used to assert their viewpoints with confidence. Develop the skills required to engage and explore emotional relationships (boyfriend/ girlfriends)

> CASE STUDY
>
> *You are the social worker for a sibling group of four children who are placed in foster care under an interim care order (an interim care order is a temporary protective order which is made by the court. It allows the local authority to share parental responsibility with the parents and make decisions, such as where the child should live, to ensure the child's welfare). The children are a baby girl aged nine months, a girl aged four years, a boy aged nine years who is nonverbal and has diagnosis of severe global developmental delay, and a boy aged fourteen years. The case is approaching the end of care proceedings, where the court will need to make final decisions and final orders about the children's care plans and where they should live in the long term. You need to obtain each child's wishes and feelings to inform the court.*
>
> ### Reflective question
>
> *Using Table 2.1 and what you know about child-focused communication, how would you plan your direct work to seek the views of each child about what they want to happen and where they want to live?*

Comment

Each child is at a different developmental stage and will have a different understanding about their experiences, and so communication will need to be tailored to their individual needs.

The 9-month-old baby is developing speech and language skills and it is accepted she cannot be explicit in her wishes and feelings. It is common for a social worker to write something like: 'it is reasonable to assume she would want to be cared for by carers who can provide her with safe and reliable care'. Whilst this may be so, there are ways of obtaining more unique wishes and feelings. Consider the following questions:

- What do you know about the baby's relationship with her mother or father?
- What have you observed about the baby's interactions and attachments during contact?
- Where else could you get information from?
- What does all this tell you and what assessments can be made about the baby's wishes and feelings?

The 4-year-old girl will have some communication skills and is likely to understand basic emotions such as happy, sad and worried. Her understanding of these can be explored by asking what makes her feel happy, etc. Pictures of these emotions can be used to support conversations about how she feels in different environments, such as in foster care, and when she sees mummy and daddy or any other relevant caregiver. It would be appropriate to ask a 4-year-old child directly about if she had the choice, where would she choose to live.

The 9-year-old boy is nonverbal and has a diagnosis of developmental delay. Communication should therefore be adapted to suit his needs, for example you could show him a happy and sad emoticon, and picture of his family home and foster home, respectively, and ask him to point at happy or sad, when asking about each home setting. His understanding of the question might be difficult to gauge and therefore in reaching assessments about his views, this will also need to be triangulated against other information. For example, are there other professional observations about his physical and emotional presentation since being in foster care? What are these and who has made them; are they from the social worker, his school or any other involved professional. What is the quality of contact?

The boy aged fourteen, due to his developmental age, is likely to understand more about the situation and give clearer views. Information about the court process can be shared with him in more detail and more direct questions about what he wants to happen can be asked. Sometimes children are explicit in their views, either wishing to return home or remain in foster care. Sometimes children at this age have divided loyalties towards their mother or father, and knowledge and understanding that the care they were being provided was harmful. Therefore, it is important to emphasise that it's okay 'not to know'. Children should be made aware that the court will listen to what they want to happen, but it is the court who will make the final decision based on the available information.

The principles of communication as discussed earlier in this chapter should be applied in your approach to communication with each child in this case example, and indeed, all communications with children and young people.

What is good communication?

Good communication involves building relationships with children and young people. The purpose of communication is to understand their day-to-day experiences. There are a range of books on effective communication which put forward techniques such as summarising, mirroring and empathetic listening. However, without the groundwork of relationship building, those important communication skills can become futile when engaging with children and young people.

When we communicate with children and young people, we are asking them to share and talk about something very personal to them, their lived experiences. Some children come straight out and share what is going on for them, others do not.

Let's do the following activity, which asks you to reflect on how you would feel being asked to share some of your more personal experiences.

ACTIVITY 2.2

Stop and think

Can you please take a moment to think about your most embarrassing moment? What happened? Why was it embarrassing? Where were you? Who was with you? What were people's responses to you? How did it make you feel? .... Now tell the person sitting next to you about it.

Comment

Looking at Activity 2.2, what were your responses to this exercise? Were you willing to tell the person sitting next to you? Why, why not?

You might have been too embarrassed to share the incident because of how it made you feel, or because of your perceptions of what others may think. Or, you may have been more willing to share your embarrassing moment if you knew the person asking the question, or if you had an interpersonal relationship with them. This is the same for children. The purpose of this exercise is to highlight that it can be difficult for children to talk about their homelife experiences. It is possible they may feel embarrassed, ashamed, scared, frightened or loyal to parents. Therefore, we need to approach communication with children and young people sensitively and empathetically, supporting them to tell us what is really happening to them. To do this well it's important to consider both how the child might feel speaking to us and how we approach communication with them.

Mostly, children and young people need to feel safe and secure, to have a sense of trust in a relationship before they are willing to talk about what life is really like for them. The role of the social worker is demanding due to the complexity of families and occasional staffing shortages which means that time can be limited. Despite these challenges, we must ensure the views of children and young people are obtained, and recorded, in assessments.

Therefore, remembering this exercise when engaging with children and young people is critical to building relationships. It allows you to take a person-centred and child-focused approach to communication by putting yourself in the child or young person's shoes. It makes you see things from the child or young persons' perspective and enables you to be sensitive to their standpoint.

So far, this chapter has already discussed the importance of child-focused communication. Therefore, the rest of this chapter looks at how we approach communication to hear the voice of the child and young person.

The three stages of good communication

Hearing the child or young person's voice is essential to safeguarding. In our interactions and exchanges, we need to draw out their lived experiences. To do this effectively, we need good communication. Not only must we be child focused, but good communication involves three stages: planning, communicating and reflecting and managing the communication.

Stage 1: Planning

The importance of planning for communication, whether it is with children, young people, parents or professionals, should never be overlooked. When planning communication, it's important to consider the following:

- Who am I communicating with?

- What is the purpose of the communication?

- How am I going to communicate?

- Where is the communication going to take place?

Who am I communicating with?

A good start to building relationships with children and young people is to reach out to them by showing a genuine interest. Before meeting a child or young person, take time to think about who they are. From the information you have, what do you know about them and their current circumstances, and how will that influence your communication with them?

Think about the child or young person's age, gender, language, culture, religion and any additional needs or disabilities they may have. Consider whether they are verbal or non-verbal. This will influence the complexity of communication used and allow communication to be pitched at the child or young person's level of understanding. Communication methods can range from observations to signs and symbols to simple sentence construction or to more complex conversations.

Take note of what you know about the child or young person's current circumstances and be mindful of this when communicating. For example, if you know it is a family where there is an absent father, don't be caught unprepared and off guard and ask, 'Does your dad live in the house?' Be mindful of cultural norms. For example, you might comment on a child losing a tooth, but don't explicitly make reference to a tooth fairy visiting. That is a cultural belief that not all people believe in. It is important to approach sensitive topics with care.

Take time to find out about something the child or young person likes or is interested in. This will demonstrate your interest in the child or young person, and can help reduce their anxieties about communicating with a new person. This information could be obtained from a parent, referrer or another involved professional such a teacher, health visitor or community nurse. It can also be obtained from the child or young person; however, remember that consent to share information from a parent is necessary to gain any additional information. You can show your interest by doing things such as finding out about a TV program me they are interested in or their favourite animal or food or colour, and taking something meaningful for them to engage with as an icebreaker. For example, if you know the child or young person likes Paw Patrol, find out about their favourite pup and take a colouring-in picture of it. Or, if they are an older child who likes Harry Potter, be creative and use this as a theme for gathering information. Some children like playing popular playground games such as 'floor is lava'. Play these with them. These efforts support relationship building and demonstrate to a child you value their experiences.

What is purpose of the communication?

In safeguarding, communication with children and young people is around understanding their wishes and feeling. It's about gaining insight into the child's or young person's perception and understanding of how they view what life is like for them. It's about unpicking what makes them feel happy and safe; and exploring what they want to stay the same or want to be different when thinking about their day-to-day experiences. To understand a child or young person, we need to understand their experiences at home. Communication with children and young people should focus on this. We will also need to explore the specific safeguarding risk factors such as neglect, sexual harm, physical harm and emotional harm.

The best chance of hearing a child's or young persons' voice is when communication is planned and has a purpose. The planning phase of communication should ask the question, 'what do I hope to achieve from this interaction or communication exchange?' It is useful to develop a session plan which contains 3–4 aims, and then sets out how you will achieve each aim. What questions will be asked? What materials, games or tools will be necessary? Now turn your attention to the case study below, to consider how you would put together a session plan in practice.

CASE STUDY

A referral has been received from a school, raising concerns that an eight-year-old girl is using sexually explicit language and has tried to touch the private parts of other children during play time. The case is progressed to an assessment due to concerns of possible sexual harm.

You are the allocated social worker and need to carry out direct work with the girl to ascertain her wishes and feelings and lived experiences.

Put together a session plan for direct work with the child. Think about:

- *What is the purpose of your direct work with this girl?*

- *What are the key questions you will ask her about?*

- *How will you ask these?*

- *What tools can you use?*

Comment

What were your key questions and communication methods in your session plan? In this case example, the key purpose of communication would be to explore where this girls' behaviours come from to inform assessments of risk of harm. Therefore, in planning for direct work, it is important to have some hypotheses, which can be tested out. For example, is this something that has happened to her, is this something she has witnessed, are these developmental exploratory behaviours? These hypotheses can form the key aims and questions.

What methods of communicating did you come up with and what factors influenced this? For communicating with younger children less direct ways of communication, such as using a role play of a tea party, or arts and crafts, might be an easier way to find out about their experiences. For older children, a game of questions and answers can be another creative means of communication. Look back to Table 2.1. A girl between ages five and thirteen can hold conversations, but may also respond to more interactive methods. One way to explore whether she is imitating sexually harmful behaviours that may have happened to her may be to give her a neutral picture of a body, and ask her if anyone has ever touched her and to mark where. What other creative means can you think of?

Session plans are helpful in preparing and guiding communication. However, it is equally important to be intuitive and flexible when engaging with children and young people. There are times when a child might not be responsive to what is prepared for the direct work. This could be for a range of reasons such as: the child or young person is feeling unwell, or doesn't want to talk to you because his or her mother badmouthed you, or the child or young person wants to talk about something else. Here the skill of 'reflecting in action' is important. Think on the spot about why the prepared plan is not working and adapt. Is it that you need to be respectful of the child's or young person's presentation and need to re-arrange the visit? Is it that there needs to be a greater focus of relationship building and you just need to play games? Is it that you need to follow the child's lead about what they are sharing? When planning communication and direct work with children and young people, it's useful to develop a broad plan of what information needs to be gained. It may be that what is planned for a later discussion needs to be brought forward.

These skills are important for communication and assessments with adults too, which is discussed in Chapter 3.

Where is the communication going to take place?

Communicating or direct work with children and young people should take place in a venue and environment that is familiar to them, and where they feel safe. It should be context specific. This is often at home. In safeguarding practice, there are statutory requirements to see the child or young person in his or her home environment. This provides opportunities to make observations of the child's or young person's attachments and behaviours in the home environment, which are important non-verbal communications when understanding the voice of the child and their day-to-day experiences. Some children and young people do not feel safe at home, and therefore whilst it's important to observe and engage with them in their home environment, it's equally important to carry out direct work with them in an alternative environment where they feel free and safe to share their wishes and feelings. This could be at school, or at a family member's address or an appropriate place in the community.

Children and young people need to be seen alone, unless there are clear reasons why this is not possible. For example, for a baby, or a child or young person who has complex health-care needs who may require a trained person with them at all times, or a disabled child who needs support with communication. This is to give children and young people an opportunity to share independently and openly. It is giving them the right to have their voice heard.

Before we consider the next stage of communication, we will now look at some common questions when it comes to overcoming barriers in order to communicate effectively with children and young people.

Q&A: OVERCOMING BARRIERS TO COMMUNICATING WITH CHILDREN AND YOUNG PEOPLE

What happens if a parent refuses for a professional to see a child alone?

The level of risk always needs to be assessed. Consider which framework of intervention under the Children Act 1989 the case is open under. Is the case open under S.17 Child In Need where there are concerns around impairment, or under S.47 Child Protection where there are concerns that the child is at risk of suffering significant harm. What is the impact if the child is not seen alone?

It is always preferable to collaboratively resolve the issue with the parent. Spend time talking to the parent, establishing the reasons why they do not want the child to be seen. Have a sound knowledge about the reasons why you need to see the child, and communicate these clearly and transparently to the parent. If no resolution is reached, be honest about any level of concern you have for the child or young person and what escalating processes may need to happen if access to the child is not given. This might include escalating to a strategy discussion, requesting a police welfare check or seeking threshold on an emergency protection order. Remind the parent that safeguarding is everybody's responsibility and that any escalating actions are due to duties and responsibilities from legal frameworks. Always seek advice from your manager.

What happens if a child or young person refuses to see a professional alone?

This happens and could be for several reasons. The child or young person might be feeling anxious or fearful or may be reluctant to engage with

(Continued)

(Continued)

a social worker (or professional) due to hearing negative views about social workers. Explain to the child or young person that it's important for you to see them, and explain the reasons why. Ask the child or young person what they would like to happen. Give them suggestions where appropriate, such as having another familiar, safe but independent adult present. Draw up an agreement together about the expectations of the communication and be clear they can leave if they become uncomfortable.

What happens if a professional does not feel safe seeing a child alone?

Professional safety must always be considered. There might be reasons a professional does not want to see a child alone, for example, a child or young person might have a history of making allegations against professionals, or the child or young person might have tendencies to act out aggressively. In these situations, it is appropriate for two professionals to be present. This could be a colleague, a safeguarding lead from a school, or a carer or a health visitor.

Practitioner safety

We have been talking about the planning stage of communication with a focus on planning your communication exchange with the child or young person. An important aspect of the planning phase is thinking about your own safety. We would like to address this point briefly. When planning to undertake direct work with children or young people, you might consider the following points:

- Find out in advance of your visits about hazards such as pets in the home.

- What do you know about the family, is it safe to visit alone? If there are high risks such as threatening behaviour, do a risk assessment with your manager about the safety of visiting alone.

- Follow departmental safety and lone working policies. Discuss this with you manager or look on the organisation's intranet for these.

Stage 2: Communicating

Communication with children and young people needs to be meaningful. The planning stage of communication emphasises the importance of preparing for communication. The communicating stage is the doing, hearing from the child about their experiences. Literature on communication suggests there is a beginning, middle and end phase to communication. This is applicable to engaging with children and young people too.

Beginning phase

At the start of discussions with children and young people, it is always ethical to explain to the child, in child-friendly terms, who you are, what your role is and why you are talking to them.

It is also useful to begin with 'icebreakers'. Often children are anxious to speak to you, and something like playing a game, or asking non-intrusive 'get to know you' questions reduce anxieties and gently ease the child into more deeper conversations. For example, I was undertaking direct work virtually with a child. The child was shy and nervous, and declined to turn his video on. I spent some time asking general questions, which helped make the child feel relaxed. The child then spontaneously turned his camera on, once some relationship building had taken place and trust in the relationship was established.

Middle phase—obtaining the child's wishes and feelings

The Department of Education sets out the Assessment Framework Triangle (2000), which forms the foundation of all assessments. It suggests domains for which information needs to be gathered and assessed, including areas around the child's individual needs, parenting they receive and environment they live in. The child's wishes and feelings about all domains should be gathered and depending on the risk factors identified there will be a heavier or lesser focus on some domains. For example, if concerns around fabricated and induced illness are raised, the social worker might spend more time talking to the child about their health and how often they go to see a doctor, how well they feel in themselves, etc. Whereas if there are concerns around domestic abuse, the social worker might spend more time talking about the parental relationship, asking questions such as: 'do mummy and daddy get on?' and 'what happens if there is a disagreement in your house?'

We will now look at how you can develop your practical skills in obtaining the child's wishes and feelings. There are a range of child-focused tools available online, within local authority resources and through key organisations such as Cafcass (https://www.cafcass.gov.uk/) which you may find useful in gathering information about the child's or young person's day-to-day life. From our experience, information about the child's health, education, emotional well-being, social opportunities, any harm they have suffered and environment they live in can be gathered from focusing questions on the child's:

   Self: What does the child like to do? What is going well in the child's life? What upsets the child about his or her life?

   Relationships: Who does the child live with? Who are the people important to the child? How does the child experience those relationships? Are they good or bad? Why?

Feelings and safety: What makes the child feel happy, sad, worried, angry etc.? What makes the child feel safe?

Wishes: What are the child's wishes for the future?

Here are some tools which we have developed to help you gather this information from the child or young person.

My House

The 'My House' tool has been developed from drawing on The Assessment Framework Triangle, which as described above guides us in what information we need to gather about the child or young person, and Signs of Safety. Signs of Safety is an approach to child protection which looks to identify strengths in individual, family and community relationships and how these can be built upon to keep children safe (signsofsafety.net). A landmark tool of the approach is 'My 3 houses' which asks children to talk about their house of worries (the harm they are experiencing), their house of good things (the strengths and things that are going well) and house of dreams (what they want to change). This is a good tool to use which has been tried and tested. The 'My House' tool amalgamates these frameworks and is effective in getting to know and understand the child or young person.

Purpose of tool: To develop a sense of the child's or young person's home life and day-to-day experiences.

How to use it: Ask the child or young person to draw a picture of his or her house. Use the features of the house to prompt discussions.

Prompts for discussion:

- Who lives in your house?

- What is it like living in your house?

    - Ask about relationships: who gets on with who?

- What are the good things at your house?

- What are the bad things at your house? (written by chimney smoke)

- Talk about the door: who do you want to come into your house? Is there anyone you don't want to come into your house? Why?

- Is there anything you would like to change about your house?

- How do you feel at your house?

Here is an example of using this tool in practice.

A variation of 'My House'

Another way to use the 'My House' tool is to prepare a worksheet for a child which has a picture of a house (to represent where and with whom they live) with different factors for a child to scale from 0 to 10 with 0 being the lowest and 10 being the highest. For example, you might ask the child to scale how happy, sad, worried or safe they feel in their house. This is useful when exploring a child's experiences across two houses.

Here is an example of what the tool could look like.

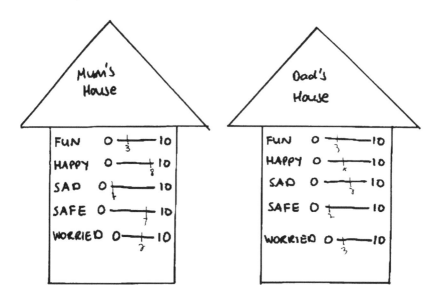

Me, my family and my community

This tool draws on systems theory and ecological perspective to gathering information about the child's lived experiences. This is the notion that the child or young person is linked, connected to, the systems around them, such as their family, friends and communities. This tool looks at the systems, or resources, around the child and how the child feels about them. This tool highlights the child's perceptions and who or what is important to the child and where they can go for support. This is important as our approach to safeguarding should take on a strengths-based approach. This is discussed in Chapter 4.

Purpose of the tool: To develop a sense of the resources around the child, and how the child feels within these.

How to use it: Ask the child to draw a circle (me), with a circle around that (my family), and a final circle around that (my community).

Prompts for discussions:

- Me: Tell me about something you're good at; something you need help with; what you like doing? What upset you?

- My Family: What do you like doing with your family? What do you like about your family? What upsets you about your family? How do you feel in your family?

- My Community: What are the places you liking going to? What are the places you don't like going to? How do you feel in these places?

Here is an example of what the tool looks like:

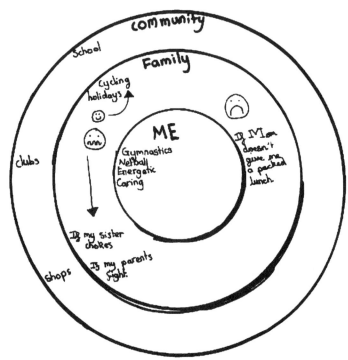

There is no right or wrong tool to use, and as you develop your practice you will find you own style of engaging with children and young people. We hope these suggestions add to your 'communication tool kit'.

End phase

It is always useful to summarise what was spoken about at the end of discussions, and to give the child an opportunity to ask questions. When the conversation ends, the child should feel listened to, feelings contained and have an idea of what will happen next.

Communicating with disabled children

In our work, we will come across children and young people who have additional needs, disabilities and difficulties communicating. This should not stop us from obtaining the voice of the child or young person. As the following activity will show, communication is more than being able to speak.

ACTIVITY **2.3**

Imagine you are thirsty. How many ways can you think of to communicate this need?

Comment

In completing this activity, you would have reflected that there are many ways of communicating. As humans, we all have the power to communicate, and therefore when working with disabled children and young people, we must remember, it is not that the child cannot communicate, but rather how are we communicating to hear the voice of the disabled child.

The planning phases of communication is even more so important when carrying out direct work with disabled children and young people. To get the best from our communication exchange we must prepare in advance and seek to understand how they communicate. For example, a child's health needs may mean they cannot form sentences, or do not have control of physical movements such as hand gestures to point, but can understand aspects of the world around them and communicate through supported systems such as eye gaze equipment or communication books. Or, in another example, a child who has difficulties hearing may be cognitively able but needs to be supported to communicate with a British sign language interpreter to make themself understood. Therefore, in planning for communication with disabled children, we need to consider the following:

- The child's level of need or disability: How does their diagnosis impact on them? For example, do they have developmental or speech delays, can they point to communicate a choice, are there physical needs, can they communicate a choice?

- The child's level of understanding: What do they understand about the world around them? Can they understand simple instructions or complex constructs? Do they use signs or symbols?

Thinking about these factors will enable meaningful communication with disabled children and young people. Their wishes and feelings will be authentic if you can support them to communicate choice.

The case example earlier in the chapter set out how using signs and symbols will be an important aid in communication with some non-verbal children. For example, showing the child a cross or tick, or happy or sad face to point to against pictures of his school, family members, activities he likes doing. This will help get a sense of what the child or young person enjoys doing and how they feel in different environments.

We will now turn to a case study to think about communicating with disabled children with more complex needs.

CASE STUDY

You are completing an assessment of need on a 13-year-old boy who has a diagnosis of autism and is blind (Every child with a disability is entitled to an assessment of need. This assesses their disability and whether they meet the need for support service such as a care package). The boy has severe developmental delays, he can make babbling sounds and displays challenging and anxious behaviours.

Reflective question

How would you gather his wishes and feelings?

Comment

Perhaps one of the most powerful ways of hearing the voice of the disabled children is through observation. It is important to observe a disabled child in different settings to understand if their behaviour is consistent or changes, and to reflect on what the behaviour is communicating to us. If a behaviour is more settled in one environment, it is likely to suggest the child is happier in that situation. If behaviour is dysregulated, it is likely to suggest something is causing stress or anxiety to the child, and it will be important to understand why, what has changed, and assess if it is causing harm.

Stage 3: Reflecting and managing communication

The third stage of communication is to reflect on the interactions and exchanges, and to consider what we do with the information gathered.

We must reflect on what the child has communicated with us, and assess what does this mean for the child? This is explained in the following case example.

CASE STUDY

A mother has an anxiety disorder and is fearful to send her child to school. When completing home visits with the child, you notice he is responsive and interested in all activities you do with him. The behaviour and nonverbal cues communicate he is bored, and his opportunities are restricted. He is looking for other learning and stimulation, and something to engage with. The child is then supported to integrate into school. When you do a further visit, he is not interested in engaging with you and spends time on his iPad.

What reflections can be made on these observations?

Comment

In this example, the child's behaviour communicates he is possibly tired from a day at school and his disinterest suggests his learning needs are now being met.

After our communication, we need to manage the information gathered. We need to think about principle of safety, confidentiality and recording. This is relevant to both communication with children and young people, and is discussed in full detail in Chapter 3.

Diversity and equality in communicating with children and young people

This section will give you an opportunity to reflect on what you have read so far and to think about the connections to diversity and equality in social work practice. Below are some examples for you to reflect and discuss if necessary, with your line manager.

| The outcome of a court decision is for Naomi, aged ten, Black British, to be placed with a white British foster carer in Norfolk. Naomi is originally from Hackney, London. | Brian is Asian, aged eleven, and is excluded from school. After, some delay he is joining a new school in a different location, that is predominately white UK. | Salina, aged fourteen, is placed with foster carers. Salina is of mixed heritage (Black/White). Her new carers are White. |

(Continued)

(Continued)

How might this decision impact on Naomi, in terms of her racial and cultural identity?	How can you work with the school to prepare for Brian to address issues of diversity and cultural difference?	How can you work with the foster carer to ensure that Salina's personal care needs are met? Are the products required for her hair and skin available locally? If not, can you identify a suitable supplier?
Having a sense of community and belonging is important. What could you do to support this basic need?	It is important that Brian feels he belongs at his new school. How would you challenge the school to address these issues?	Her new family, include siblings who are aged seven and sixteen. How would you work with the siblings and Salina to deal with cultural differences?

In safeguarding, we need to ensure that we meet the cultural and diversity needs of children and young people. However, there may be times when, for example, a race, religious or cultural match is not available. In this situation, the child's need to be placed in a safe and caring environment where their well-being is promoted must be prioritised. The principles of communication as discussed in this chapter will be important in helping children and young people understand their circumstances, and hearing from them how their cultural and diversity can still be promoted. For example, if Salina tells you she is a practicing Christian and likes to go to church on a Sunday. What arrangements can be made to meet her religious need?

Communicating with children and young people and a remote way of working

The way we communicate with children and young people is changing. COVID-19 has forced our exchanges and interactions to be remote. Instead of face-to-face visits, it more common to do our direct work with children and young people on video platforms and through a screen. There is now a bigger question to be debated around whether remote ways of working will replace face-to-face visits, and whether this promotes safe practice.

This is an emerging issue in safeguarding and social work practice, where research and practice development are ongoing. When thinking about the issues, there are advantages and disadvantages to both methods of communication. Indeed, children and young people have become more adept at using devices to communicate as it has become more akin to a social norm, and those aged ten and older are often more comfortable communicating this way as we move into a digital world. Some of the difficulties in remote working include children turning their camera off and walking away from screens. It is difficult to guarantee whether they are on their own and expressing their wishes and feelings freely, and a screen cannot replace real-observation. For example, seeing and smelling a home environment could be pivotal in assessing the level of neglect, which would be missed when working remotely.

Remote ways of working does not replace the human connection of face-to-face working, however good and effective communication has taken place when working remotely too. Remote ways of working have, and will, become part of our social work toolkit. Going forward, we will need to make judgements about when to carry out a remote visit and when to carry out a face-to-face visit. We will now consider what factors influence this decision-making.

What factors should be considered when deciding to do a face-to-face or remote visit?

ADASS (Association of Directors of Adult Social Services) North East have devised a defencible decision-making tool for virtual visits (December 2020) which is being used in adults, social care in North East England. This can be found on the Social Work England YouTube channel at https://www.youtube.com/watch?v=-9GlepXWlGM (25 March 2021). As remote working becomes integrated into social work practice, social workers in both children and adults' services are likely to need to provide a rational for undertaking either an in person or virtual visit. Drawing on this adult services tool as well as our own experience, we have come up with some question prompts to support your thinking and decision-making on whether to carry out an in-person or virtual visit. These are prompts and should not replace discussion and guidance from your manager.

	Low risk—indicates 'virtual visit'	High risk—indicates 'in person' visit
Is the person known to children's services?	Case is open. The child has been seen recently by either social worker or partner agency.	Child/family not known. New safeguarding referral from parent/ partner agency. New safeguarding concern in open case.
What is the purpose of the visit?	e.g. Planned 1:1 session for purposes of completing a parenting assessment Review meeting Obtaining wishes and feelings where there is an established relationship. Professionals meeting	e.g. Statutory visit Direct observation of behaviour/contact/ relationships Assessment of new risk
When was the child last seen, and by whom?	Child seen recently by professional with updated feedback on risk	Not seen recently by professional

(Continued)

(Continued)

	Low risk—indicates 'virtual visit'	High risk—indicates 'in person' visit
What is the current risk assessment?	Low risk	High risk
What is the age of the child/children?	8 + more likely to engage meaningfully and concentrate with technology	0–8 years more likely to have difficulties engaging with technology
Does the child have any additional needs?	No	Yes, e.g. Additional needs such as autism where observation important
Does the parent/carer have any additional needs?	No	Yes
How do parents/child wish to engage with you?	Virtually	Face to face
Is there technology available to support a remote visit that allows for participation?	Yes	No
Are you in good health or poorly?	Poor health	Good health
Are parents/carers in good health	Poor health	Good health

TOP TIPS FOR EFFECTIVE COMMUNICATION WHEN WORKING REMOTELY

Our approach to communicating with children and young people as set out in this chapter does not change when working remotely. We still need to develop relationships with children which enable them to feel safe to share their experiences. We still need to be child-focused in our communication. We still need to plan our communication. The same communication tools to draw out the children's experiences can be used. Therefore, it is more practical for us to share best practice tips with you.

- *Know how to use technology and test this out.*

- *Think confidentiality. Direct work now entails sharing computer screens. Ensure any confidential documents are saved, closed and out of view.*

- *Block out distractions such as closing your emails.*

- *Privacy: ensure you are in a private place where you cannot be overheard or overlooked.*

Chapter summary

- We have an ethical and legal mandate to hear the voice of the child. This means we need to engage children and young people to hear what their feelings, views and future hopes are, and to record these in assessments.

- The key principles of communication with children and young people are child centred, context specific, encouragement, values their experiences and promotes discovery.

- Communication should be child-focused. We must ensure the child and young person can understand and relate to what we are sharing with them, and that what is shared with them is in line with their developmental and emotional needs.

- Good and effective communication involves planning communication, communicating and reflecting on communication.

- There are a wide range of tools to engage with disabled and non-verbal children.

YOUR LEARNING JOURNEY

This chapter has provided you with 'how to' tips to communicate with children and young people by developing your practice skills around what factors needs to be considered when you approach communication with children and young people and providing you with direct practice tools to use in your communication with them. Below are a few questions for you to consider.

- *After reading this chapter, what have you learned about communicating with children and young people?*

- *How will you apply this in your practice?*

- *Use one tool discussed in this chapter in your work with children this week. Reflect on:*

  - *How did the child respond to this?*

  - *Was it effective in getting the child's wishes and feelings?*

- *Research and use another direct practice tool.*

Chapter 3

Communicating with adults and professionals

Chapter objectives

This chapter seeks to answer these questions:

- Who are the adults we communicate with and why do we communicate with them?

- What is the challenge in safeguarding practice and how to challenge adults and professionals?

- How to communicate with challenging adults?

- What do we do with the information from our communication?

Introduction

Listening to the voice of the child ensures that their wishes are known and our decision-making has been informed by their views. We know that safeguarding children is everyone's responsibility, and this requires social workers to communicate with adults. This includes the parents/carers of children that require our intervention, and the other professionals involved in the child's life, such as schoolteachers, the health visitor, school nurse and general practitioner, to name but a few. Put simply, we must communicate with adult carers and other professionals if we are to identify actual or likelihood of risk and protect children and young people.

As part of our work with children and families, we will need to communicate with adults in a variety of different contexts and demonstrate knowledge about our role and responsibility. Communicating with adults as part of the safeguarding process is essential, and this often requires the social worker to confidently challenge adults and professionals to ensure the child's care plan is achieved and improves the lived experiences of the child and young person. When communicating with the adults and professionals involved in the child's or young person's life you should be respectful and decisive about what happens to the information recorded, as well as how you intend to effectively safeguard and protect.

The Social Work England professional standards identifies a specific standard on communication (2.5, 3.10 and 5.6, https://www.socialworkengland.org.uk/standards/standards-guidance/professional-standards-guidance/, accessed 25 May 2021).

> Communication is at the heart of effective professional relationships in social work and is the means of informing, supporting and listening to people. A social worker will tailor the way they communicate with people and consider factors such as age, disability, experience, culture, belief and intellectual impairment when assessing communication. Information should always be given in a form, language and manner that people can understand. It is important that social workers reflect their considerations around communication in their records and review them appropriately.

This chapter will consider the range of adults and professionals a social worker might communicate with as part of their work, and outlines the importance of communicating effectively with adults and other professionals.

Who are the adults we communicate with and why do we communicate with them?

The report *Complexity and challenge: A triennial analysis of SCRs 2014-2017: Final report* (Department of Education, 2020) highlighted several themes from their review of 368 SCRs (Serious Case Reviews) of children affected by serious and fatal child neglect and maltreatment. These themes are particularly pertinent to how we communicate with adults and professionals and highlights why we need to do this effectively:

- Most serious and fatal maltreatment continue to take place within the family, involving parents and family members.

- Not all children involved in SCRs had direct involvement with the child protection system. Therefore working with adults and professionals is crucial for minimising risk.

- Building positive relationships with adults within the child's family is a key channel to enhance protective factors.

- The family and wider community are an important source of information and support during the social work intervention stage. For example, the literature on safeguarding tells us about the importance of absent fathers.

- Effective multi-agency working requires professionals to consider the language used because collectively it has the potential to both support and hinder effective safeguarding. Adults and professionals have a shared responsibility in agreeing the plan, understanding the language used and ensuring the focus remains on the child's needs.

Communicating with adults and professionals is different from that of the child who is subject of a safeguarding concern for several reasons:

- The adult and professional has an important role in helping to keep the child and young person safe. As an adult they have a responsibility and duty to protect and safeguard young people. This means that communication with adults must recognise firstly they have a role to play and more importantly will be held accountable by their agency, statutory and legal duties and society at large if they minimise or are ambiguous about the risks faced by young people.

- As adults we need to be skilled at understanding both verbal and non-verbal communication by adults and other professionals as together they can give insight into how people are feeling and provide opportunities to develop positive working relationships.

- We are also accountable to children and young people; this means that when we communicate with adults we should always represent the voice and views of the child and be open and transparent about the plans and possible outcomes.

- A focus on the facts and views and wishes of adults/professionals is crucial but this should be respectful of cultural and diversity factors within the family.

CASE STUDY

Consider the notes from a social worker who conducted a home visit below:

I conducted a home visit and was at the home with Mrs Smith and Jenny (aged eighteen months) for one and half hours. During that time, Jenny did not approach her mother or interact with her physically or verbally. At one stage she looked under the couch and found an old bottle that she started to drink from. She came over to me and sat on my lap to finish her bottle. Jenny was very wet and it soaked onto my lap whilst she was sitting here. I mentioned this to Mrs Smith who did not change her during my visit. She did not speak to or approach Jenny during my visit.

There could be several things happening in this situation and at the moment all you have done is describe what you observed.

(Source: *Strengthening Assessment and Interventions, 2013, Northamptonshire County Council*).

CASE STUDY *continued*

Reflective questions

Having read the above case notes:

- *What are you concerned or worried about?*
- *What are the gaps in information?*
- *What is your hypothesis about what is going on?*

Comment

In this case example, there can be many things happening. For example, is Mrs Smith experiencing depression or does Jenny have a hearing impairment? In our communication with adults, we need to seek to understand what is going on and then support and encourage adults to respond to their children's safety and welfare needs.

What is challenge in safeguarding practice?

Parents or carers of children and young people, and professionals are all unique. They have their own set of ideas, beliefs, experiences and way of doing things. This is their human right, and their views should be respected and understood. However, when these are assessed to cause harm to a child or young person, intervention is required. The welfare of the child is paramount and therefore, there are times that it is necessary to challenge: to challenge a parent's style or way of parenting; or to challenge a professional when there is a difference of opinion about what is in a child's best interest.

In a safeguarding context, 'challenge' means to open up a discussion and invite another individual to reflect on their thoughts and actions and to consider a new way of doing things which will make things better for the child or young person. It is inviting someone to do things differently. Therefore, the skill of challenging is an important part of communicating with adults. We need to have the courage to tell a parent, carer or professional that what they are doing is harmful and give them opportunities to change. We must practice with transparency and integrity and inform parents of safeguarding concerns, except when doing so would place the child at further risk of significant harm. It would be unfair on the parent to arrive, for example, at a Child Protection Conference (a meeting which discusses safeguarding concerns for the child and family) without already being told what professionals are worried about. Whether the adult or parent accepts or shows insight into the concerns or not is a matter for assessment. Safeguarding concerns always centre around an adult's behaviours and their capacity to parent a child safely. This cuts to the core of human nature. Therefore, how we challenge needs to be undertaken with respect and honesty.

ACTIVITY 3.1

Can you think of a time when you had to challenge someone, where you had to point out that their way of doing something was incorrect and support them to do it in a different way?

- *How did you do this?*

- *Did the person change?*

- *What worked?*

- *What did you learn?*

Let's look at Activity 3.1, which will start to develop your thinking in how we can challenge adults.

Comment

We hope that you realised in your reflections that there is a balance to be struck between highlighting the negatives and promoting the positives. This is the same in safeguarding practice. Repeat conversations on what parents are doing wrong can be draining, demoralising and a barrier to achieving change. Using a strengths-based approach, which identifies an individual's strengths and builds on these to motivate and bring about change, is likely to yield a more positive response by parents and improve outcomes for children and young people.

One approach to giving feedback is telling a parent something they are doing well, telling them about the concern and then telling them about another thing they are doing well.

How to challenge parents and motivate change

In our communication with adults, we need to support them to accept the need for change in their parenting style. Before we consider how to do this, it is important to first understand models of change as this informs our assessment of change, and how we approach communication with adults to motivate change.

The Cycle of Change model

The Cycle of Change model (Prochaska and Di Clemente, 1982) puts forward different stages which need to be passed through in achieving change. These include the following:

- Pre-contemplation (no awareness there is problem that needs changing)

- Contemplation (developing an awareness of the need to change)

- Determination (getting ready to change), action (doing the change)
- Maintenance (keeping up new behaviours)
- Relapse (falling back into old ways of doing things).

The Cycle of Change model has the premise that for change to be achieved, there needs to be acknowledgement that there is a problem, acceptance of responsibility in it, determination to change, engagement with support services to change behaviours and then demonstration of new, improved behaviour over a sustained period. It therefore follows that in safeguarding, our responsibilities are to make adults aware of the welfare concern for their child/children, motivate them to change and provide the intervention or services to support change.

Practice tips on how to communicate to motivate change

A large part of communication with adults and carers of children is to raise awareness of the need to change. Here are some ideas of how you might go about this in practice:

- **Always seek to understand the parent's perspective of the safeguarding concern being raised.**

Parents and carers are partners in the assessment process. We need to understand their awareness of the concern being raised, and their understanding and explanation of it. Ask questions which allow you to gain this insight. Examples of questions might include the following:

What do you think the professionals are worried about?

Or if there is a specific concern:

Did you notice any marks or bruises on Stacey? Can you tell me how she got these?

- **Name the concern, and evidence it with an example.**

Good safeguarding practice is evidence based. The evidence of concerns will come from observations and records from a range of professionals, including your own observations of family dynamics and interactions or direct work with children, as well as notifications from the police, health professionals and schools or other professionals involved with a family or members of the community. If parents are not being forthcoming about the issue, be clear and transparent in telling them where you have got the information and why you are worried. For example:

I am worried that there are problems in your relationship with Sam. Danny's school have reported that Danny often falls asleep in class. When I asked Danny about this, he said he struggles to get to sleep because he often hears his mummy and daddy shouting, and then his mummy crying. Is this something that happens? Can you tell me about it?

Or

> *The medical report from the dietician shows Jamal's weight is dropping. Why do you think that is happening?*

- **Be thoughtful about how information is presented.**

Ultimately, the result of communication and engagement with parents should bring about change, supporting parents to understand why their way of doing things is causing harm, and empowering them to make positive changes to parenting. Something simple, like counting the number of missed hospital appointments, or police calls-outs over a period of time helps parents concep-tualise the wider picture of the concerns and the impact. Remember to use simple language or visual aids for adults with learning difficulties.

- **Enable the parent to be child focused and to think about how the concern is impacting on the child.**

This is key. No matter the harm caused, most parents deeply love their child/children. Asking questions that involved parents putting themselves in their child/children's shoes can be powerful in bringing about change. For example:

> *How do you think Casey feels when he hears you shouting in the night?*

Or

> *The doctors have said Jayden is clinically obese. What do you think this is like for Jayden? (question prompts might be: Do his clothes fit him? Can he walk where he needs to? Can he keep up with his peers?) Put the risks to the parents and ask them how they will stop this from happening.*

Now let's turn our attention to the following case example to look at how we can apply the concept of challenge in our communication with adults.

CASE STUDY

You are a social worker completing an assessment due to concerns around domestic violence. You undertake a home visit to gather information from a mother. The mother tells you she is no longer in a relationship with the father and has not seen him since the relationship ended three weeks ago. She tells you she wants nothing to do with him. Upon your return to the office, you receive a police notification detailing that the police were called on the day before the home visit by a neighbour as there was lots of shouting heard. It is recorded that there was a verbal altercation, alongside some pushing and shoving between the mother and the father. The children were present and distressed.

Reflective question

How would you discuss this with the mother?

Comment

The mother has not been honest with you and there are live concerns that the children are exposed to frightening adult behaviours. You need to challenge her about this and find out more to thoroughly assess the risk to the children. It is good practice to give her a further opportunity to be honest with you. You could ring her up and say, 'I am following up on our discussions, was there anything further you wanted to tell me about your relationship with the children's father?' If she still does not come forward, an appropriate way is to use the technique of naming the concern and evidencing it with an example, as described above.

Motivational Interviewing

Motivational Interviewing has become a popular and effective interviewing approach used in safeguarding to support and promote change. It involves the worker having an empathetic, non-confrontational style of communicating, and empowers people to change by drawing out their own meaning, importance and capacity for change (Miller and Rollnick, 2013; Maclean and Harrison, 2015). There are four fundamental processes to Motivational Interviewing:

- *Engaging:* this is about establishing an effective working relationship with the parent or caregiver.

- *Focusing:* identifying collaboratively what the problem is and what needs to change.

- *Evoking:* supporting the person to come up with their own reasons and motivations as to why change is necessary. MacLean and Harrison (2015) summarise techniques that can be used to do this including educating, providing information on the impact or effects of risk, exploring the benefits and costs of current lifestyle choices and alternative lifestyle choice if they were to change and exploring barriers to change and how to overcome them.

- *Planning:* embedding a commitment to change and exploring how change can be achieved.

The success of Motivational Interviewing lies within the approach to communication, which must be non-judgemental, collaborative, show acceptance regardless of views and is compassionate (Miller and Rollnick, 2013). The communication skills of open questions, affirmations, reflections, summarising and careful use of language are foundational to the communication exchange and motivational interviewing process. We would direct you to the following full texts to find out more about this approach:

- Miller, W R and Moyers, T B (2017) Motivational interviewing and the clinical science of Carl Rogers. *Journal of Consulting and Clinical Psychology*, 85 (8), pp. 757–766.

- Miller, W R and Rollnick, S (2013) Motivational interviewing: helping people to change (3rd Ed.). Guilford Press.

- Miller and Rollnick (2017) Ten things MI is not Miller, W R and Rollnick, S (2009) Ten things that MI is not. *Behavioural and Cognitive Psychotherapy*, 37, pp. 129–140.

REFLECTIVE QUESTION

Now that you know a little bit about Motivational Interviewing, look back to the case study. How could Motivational Interviewing be used to support the mother to act protectively towards her children?

Comment

It will be important to *engage* the mother and find out more about the context of the domestic incident. It may be that the father turned up, unwelcomed, and the mother needs support obtaining a non-molestation order to prevent further such incidents from happening. It may be that the mother invited the father over. In this scenario further Motivational Interviewing techniques will need to be used to *evoke* change. This could include telling her how the children say they feel; giving her information about the impact of domestic abuse on outcomes for children; signposting her to domestic abuse support services.

In cases of domestic violence, as social workers we cannot tell parents who they can and can't be in a relationship with. However, we have a duty to intervene when the dynamics of the relationship are causing harm to the children. However difficult, the parents will need to make a choice over prioritising the safety needs of their children or their own needs to be in a relationship.

How to communicate with challenging adults

Safeguarding is everybody's responsibility, and all professionals are equal stakeholders in this. Our communication with professionals is mostly around sharing information about the risks and protective factors for children and families and being accountable for carrying out the support and interventions that are being provided to the family. There are times when it is necessary to challenge other professionals or colleagues too. This might be because we feel they are not meeting responsibilities in either a Child in Need or Child Protection Plan, or where there is a difference of opinion. When doing this you should always do the following:

- Have a confidential discussion with the person.

- Seek to understand the reasons for your view or recommendations. And the reasons for the other person's view or recommendations.

- Reflect on the impact of each view on the child or decision. Is this significant? Does it place the child or young person at risk of harm? Can a safe outcome be reached?

- If no resolution is achieved, escalate it to your manager.

- Follow organisation policy on escalation.

Having read the above guidance on the appropriate course of action when challenging other professional, now consider the following case study and how you might approach this situation.

CASE STUDY

A group of professionals have been working with a family for a substantial amount of time. One of the issues is the child's weight gain, which is long-standing. The child is now obese and there are direct impacts on his physical health. An action of the intervention plan is for the school nurse to discuss healthy eating with the child and parents, and complete weekly weigh-ins to monitor weight gain or weight loss. The school nurse becomes disillusioned as he has been working with the family on the same issue for a substantial time. He stops his work.

Reflective question

How would you deal with this as the social worker assigned to this case?

Comment

The professional does not have the option of walking out—they have a duty of care to this child. Remind them of this responsibility and where necessary escalate to his line manager.

Communicating with challenging parents

In safeguarding practice, the word *challenge or challenging* is used often and with two different meanings. We have already talked about challenge as a verb, and the need for us in our communication with adults to raise awareness of a safeguarding concern and encourage carers of children to do things differently to keep their children happy, healthy and safe. We will now talk about challenging as an adjective, and look at how adults might be challenging in their responses to you in a safeguarding role.

When we communicate with adults, they might present with aggressive and hostile behaviours, they might be anxious and need regular reassurance or they might be non-engaging and non-contactable. To achieve best outcomes for children, we need to overcome these barriers to communication. When communicating with adults it is helpful to do the following:

- Set boundaries and expectations about your communication at your first meeting. This is important as when there is concern about rude or aggressive behaviour, you can refer to what was initially agreed about communication.

- For safety, complete joint home visits when risks are identified around hostility and aggression. Inform your manager after any visit so they know you are safe.

- Use emails to communicate if phone calls result in high levels of verbal abuse and a loss of focus on the issues for the child.

- It is okay to end a telephone conversation or leave a home visit if an adult is being aggressive or hostile. However, before doing so, remind the adult of what was agreed about this type of behaviour, if no change is made, leave. Remain calm and level-headed and do not rise to the behaviour.

- Do not take things personally. Most insults are directed at the profession and not the individual.

- Always seek support from your manager or practice supervisor.

- Sometimes communicating with parents can be time-consuming, for example as a social worker you might experience multiple phone calls a day from one parent. It is important to be responsive to parents, but set boundaries on when you will respond to them. Safeguarding concerns should always be prioritised, but if parents are calling repeatedly for non-urgent requests, set time aside weekly to respond to them, and inform the parents of this.

What do we do with information from our communication?

Chapter 2 focuses on communication with children and young people. This chapter focuses on communication with adults, including carers of children and professionals. When we look at this closely, we hope you can see that there is a difference. Our communication with children is about seeking to understand their lived experiences. Our communication with adults is about ensuring the safety of children. With parents or carers of children we are seeking to understand why they do what they do, and in our communication we must motivate them to take up their safeguarding responsibilities and parent in a way that will promote their child's welfare. With professionals we communicate to share information about a child and adult to ensure a child's welfare. A large part of safeguarding is communicating, and therefore we need to consider what we do with the information gathered and gleaned from our communications.

Ultimately our communication culminates in an assessment. This is discussed in Chapter 4.

However, we must remember that in our communication, the child, young person or adult is giving us important data, their personal views and understanding of a situation, and details of their day-to-day experiences. At all times, this information needs to be handled professionally, sensitively and safely.

Keeping children and families safe

Safeguarding should be at the forethought of all communication and if information is disclosed which raises a concern that a child, or adult, is at risk of harm, safeguarding procedures should immediately be followed. This could include making a referral for specialist services or making a safeguarding referral to a Local Authority for either a child or an adult. If the case for the child is already open to the local authority, have discussions with a manager around whether processes need to be escalated under S47 of the Children Act 1989 and or emergency protection orders sought. Let's turn to the following case study to think about what this means in practice.

CASE STUDY

You are the allocated social worker to a boy aged fourteen years. He has a diagnosis of Global Developmental Delay and his speech, language and learning are significantly delayed. In the family are the boy and his mother, who is a single parent. The family is new to the area and the boy is awaiting a school placement in a specialist provision. The family has been engaging with you, but you have been unable to reach them by telephone for a number of days now, so you undertake an unannounced home visit at midday. When you arrive, you struggle to rouse anyone. Eventually mother comes to the door, the curtains are drawn, the house is dark, she is in her pyjamas and looks like she hasn't changed her clothes for a few days, and there are piled-up dishes in the kitchen. Mother discloses she has recently suffered the death of a family member living in her home country, which is abroad. This is significantly impacting on her. You observe she is noticeably low in mood with little motivation to do anything. She tells you she spends most her time sleeping or sitting on the sofa. And what's more, you are unclear what level of supervision, care and interaction/engagement is being provided by the mother to her son who is out of school and has a high level of support needs.

Reflective question

Considering what the mother has told you and what you have observed, what would you do with this information gathered from this visit?

Comment

The communication gathered from this case scenario raises risks for the child and adult's immediate welfare. You should always discuss these with a manager as a first response. Necessary key actions likely to come from this case scenario could be making a referral to adult mental health services to provide assessment, intervention and support to the mother, as well as considering how can the child be safe and his well-being needs met. You could be required to complete an assessment on whether there are any family members who can look after the child in the interim. You may need to consider whether a care package of support is needed whereby carers can go into the home for period of time daily to ensure the boy has access to food, his personal care needs are being met and he is being provided with necessary interaction and learning. You may also consider a short stay in a respite unit, or placement in foster care under a Section 20 Agreement of the Children Act 1989. This is when a child is placed in local authority care under voluntary consent by the parent. You may also need to consider whether a strategy discussion is required to consider whether the case needs to be managed under a more protective framework, such as Child Protection.

Confidentiality

Communication is confidential. This means, it is privileged to the person sharing the information, and should be kept private. Confidentiality should only be broken when there is a risk of harm to the person sharing the information, or another person. A lack of information sharing has been, and continues to be, a key finding for many serious case reviews. Consequently, Working Together Guidance makes provisions that when working under child protection procedures, consent to share information is overridden. It is good practice to always seek permission to share information from the adult. When this is not possible, it is necessary to be clear about the reasons for which information is being shared and what outcome this will have on the child, and importantly, record this. As a guide, share what is relevant and only share this to relevant people. It is good practice to share these boundaries of information sharing at the start of any communication with an adult.

Confidentiality also needs to be understood and practiced within the systems and organisations that key workers work in: All organisations have their own policies and procedures for recording communication and contact with parents and professionals. And therefore, communication with children, parents and professionals is confidential to the organisation in which it is stored. The recorded information should only be accessed by the allocated worker and team manager, and at times duty worker when the allocated worker is not available and is responding to a request. Adults have the right to access the information an organisation holds on them at any time through making a request to access their records.

Now that we have discussed some of the issues, let's turn our attention to how we can apply these principles of confidentiality in communication and information sharing when safeguarding children and young people.

CASE STUDY

You are the allocated social worker. The case is before the Family Court due to safeguarding concerns and that the care being provided to the children by their parents is causing them harm. In considering care arrangements and where the children should live either in the short or long term, the Local Authority has a duty to explore all possible placements, including placement with family and friends. You are completing a viability assessment on the paternal grandparents who have put themselves forward as potential cares. A viability assessment is a preliminary assessment to determine whether there is merit in pursuing a full assessment.

Reflective questions

- *How much information about the safeguarding concerns can you share with the potential carers when undertaking the viability assessment?*

- *Should all assessments and legal papers be shared at this stage?*

Comment

In this example you need to weigh up two things: that the information you hold about a child or parent is confidential and balance this against safeguarding responsibilities. The potential carers will need to know what the Local Authority is worried about as their understanding of the concerns and capacity to protect need to be assessed in the viability assessment. However, confidentiality needs to be respected. It is not appropriate to share the full details of the safeguarding concerns until there is a recommendation that a further, more in-depth assessment is completed. Even then, confidentiality must be respected. The parents may consent for the assessment and court papers to be shared; they may not. They may wish for some information to be redacted. You will then need to decide what is the relevant information that needs to be shared to allow for a thorough and comprehensive risk assessment of the potential carers, and make arrangements for that information to be disclosed. If agreement cannot be reached, it may be a matter for the court to decide what information is disclosed to the potential carers.

Confidentiality needs to be considered both in terms of how we handle the information that is gained and in accessing information from partner agencies and sharing communication. This is explained in the following case example.

You are a social worker completing a children and family assessment. There are concerns around the mother's mental health where she has a diagnosis of Emotionally Unstable Personality Disorder and has recently made a suicide attempt. She has been reviewed by a mental health professional. You need access to the information from this review to inform your risk assessment. The mother refuses for a copy of her mental health assessment to be shared with you. The mental health practitioner is reluctant to share the report as the mother has explicitly told him she does not consent for this to be shared, and she has threatened to make a complaint.

Reflective question

How would you respond to this situation?

Comment

In this case example, the issues are around whether the communication the mother has shared with the mental health practitioner, which is confidential to that communication exchange, should be shared. You will need to think about whether it is proportionate and necessary to the child's welfare for this confidentiality to be broken. The straight answer is yes. This information will undoubtedly aid your understanding of the mother's mental health presentation and what this means for the child's welfare. However, if the case is open under Child in Need, which is voluntary, the mental health service is not obliged to share their report. If the case is open under child protection where a strategy discussion has taken place, the mental health service will have duties to share the report, as per Working Together Guidance. It is good practice to understand the mother's resistance to information sharing. An unreasoned refusal to give consent can increase safeguarding risks and tip the case into child protection enquiries as there is no clear understanding of the risks to the child, and the information is required to inform whether the child is safe or not. It may be that there is a certain piece of information the mother does not want shared, such as an adverse childhood experience. A discussion about this, where you agree what the mental health practitioner can share with you, can resolve the issue where confidentiality is respected, and the child is protected.

Recording communication

As a social worker you will be required to work with a range of adults in different contexts such as a telephone discussions with professionals, home visits with families, Child in Need meetings, child protection conferences and Child Looked After reviews. Regardless of the context, when working with adults and other professionals we should prepare an agenda in advance so all parties are clear about what will be discussed. A written record of any meeting should be made available to all parties attending the meeting.

It is good practice to record all communication in a timely manner. Good recordings should be factual, demonstrate professional judgement and put across all viewpoints. We need to be mindful that at any point a Subject Access Request can be made, and recognise the importance of fair representation of communication with adults and other professionals.

Recording communication is important because it provides a written account of an event which took place, and evidence for the work undertaken with the family. Recordings will show patterns of behaviour and build a picture of what is going on for the family marking progress and regression and allowing assessment. Case recording is also important to case audits, which allows standards of practice to be reviewed and ensures safe decisions for children are made.

Good recording is essential to case continuity. It tells the story of what the assessed risks and protective factors are to the child and young person, and what actions have been undertaken and what actions are outstanding. This is of utmost importance when issues come up on a case and the allocated social worker is not there to respond to them, such as when on leave or out of hours. It allows safe decisions to continue to be made for the child or young person. If recording is not up-to-date, there can be grave implications for the child or young person. Let us consider this in the following case scenario:

Imagine you are the allocated social worker to a child who lives with his mother; parents are separated. You are involved due to a risk of relationship breakdown between the child and his mother. The father lives in a different county and you receive a phone call from the local authority where the father resides to say they were previously involved as the father has been physically abusive towards his son. You have not had time to update the system of this risk. Overnight the child and mother have an argument where the child is physically aggressive towards his mother and the police are called. The police assess mother and son need a cooling-off period and are looking if there is anyone who can have the child overnight. The police call out-of-hours social work team, who do some checks. The information that the father is a risk to the child is not available to them. From what they can see on the system, the child has a father, and he is someone familiar to the child whom the child can stay with. The lack of recoding has resulted in the child being placed in a potentially unsafe environment.

This scenario speaks for itself. Social workers are always under pressure but the importance of recording is a must.

Diversity and equality in communicating with adults

'Diversity' is the factor that makes us who we are. It refers to our race, religion, culture, language, ethnicity and gender. Diversity is our individual likes and interests and how our values, beliefs and experiences shape us. What are your diversity factors? Take some time to reflect on these.

- What are your values, beliefs and experiences?
- Do these impact on how you engage and approach communication with adults?

In safeguarding, we need to be aware of diversity factors, and to remain neutral and non-judgemental in our approach to communication with adults. Thinking about this, how would you respond in the following scenarios, which you are likely to come across:

How will you engage with a parent who is a head teacher or nurse?	If you are a single parent, how will you engage with a parent that is a single parent?	How will your faith-based beliefs impact on your interactions with someone of a different faith?
Would perceptions of education, class and reputation impact on your communication with them?	Will you be more lenient or critical in your engagement and assessment of safeguarding concerns?	Recognise that differences relating to our beliefs is normal and promote inclusivity for all. Think about strategies you can use to keep the child/young person at the centre of your interactions. Ask yourself what does the young person want?

From reflecting on these diversity and equality practice issues, two important comments can be made:

- Safeguarding cuts across race, religion, culture, language, ethnicity and gender.
- In our communication with adults, we need to be aware of our individual diversity factors and set aside these biases. We must be professionally curious and ask questions to understand the other's adult's viewpoint, in a non-threatening and non-judgemental manner. This enables risk assessment and for us to truly advocate for the child.

Communicating with adults and a remote way of working

COVID-19 has impacted social work practice. Remote ways of working are being integrated into how we do social work and engage and communicate with children, adults and professionals. Chapter 2 discusses this in more detail and provides some practice tips for undertaking remote work with children. These also apply to communicating remotely with adults. We will now turn to the following activity to reflect on how we can further improve our communication with adults when working remotely.

ACTIVITY **3.2**

Child protection conference practice during COVID-19: Rapid Consultation (Sep–Oct 2020) (Baginsky et al., 2020) is a recent research publication which investigates the impact and experiences of remote child protection conferences for professionals and families. Read the full report, and then reflect on the following questions. The report can be found at:

https://www.nuffieldfjo.org.uk/resource/child-protection-conference-practice-covid-19.

Reflective question

The research identifies the benefits and disadvantages of remote child protection conferences.

What are these?

The research makes findings that professionals had different experiences to families: professionals preferred remote conferences whereas families would have preferred face-to-face conferences. Some families felt they were restricted by technology which limited their engagement; they neither understood what was happening nor felt supported to engage fully and fairly in the process. Concerns around safety were raised as a finding, for example, in cases of domestic abuse there were concerns around who was in the room and could someone be in danger due to what is heard/said; and, concerns whether children are within earshot, hearing issues that are not age appropriate or being exposed to heightened emotions from adults because of conversations. Confidentiality was a further concern, in terms of the potential to dial into a different meeting; who is in the household and listening in, where is the family member joining the video call from? There were also finding and whether proper accommodations have been made for families with disabilities.

- Whilst these findings are specific to child protection conferences, how can you take these learning forward in your day-to-day communication and interactions with adults? Reflect and discuss with your line manager.

Chapter summary

- Communication with adults, both parents or carers or children and professionals is essential to safeguarding.

- Communication with professionals is about information sharing and professional accountability.

- Communication with parents is about motivating them to take up their safeguarding responsibilities. We do this by challenge.

- 'To challenge' is to raise an awareness of a problem and invite a parent to consider a new way of doing things which will allow their child to be happy, healthy and safe.

- Motivational Interviewing is an effective approach in communication with adults to evoke change.

- Practice tips for working with challenging parents.

- In our communication exchanges, with either children, parents and professionals, we must think about safety, confidentiality and recording.

YOUR LEARNING JOURNEY

This chapter has focused on communication with adults, including parents or carers of children, and professionals in partner agencies. We have provided you with practice tips on how to support parents, and at times professionals, to take up their safeguarding responsibilities to ensure children are happy and safe. Stop and think:

- *From reading this chapter, what have you learned about communicating with adults including parents and professionals?*

- *How can you apply this in your practice?*

As a closing thought on this subject, be mindful that the teams and organisations you will work for are included in the adults we need to communicate with. You are likely to come across a scenario where you disagree with either your team manager of senior manager about what is in the best interests of children and young people, and what actions or services should be provided to them.

- *How can you prepare to deal with this scenario?*

- *What knowledge skills and behaviours will you use to advocate for the child?*

Chapter 4

Assessment: managing risk and decision-making

Chapter objectives

This chapter seeks to answer these questions:

- Why do we undertake assessments?

- What makes a good assessment?

- How to use our Safeguarding Assessment and Decision-Making Tool to reach safe decisions for children and young people?

- What is a report and how to write a good report?

Introduction

Assessments are undertaken when there are concerns about the level of care being provided to a child or young person. The purpose of an assessment is to consider how an event, home environment or the behaviour of a significant other is impacting on the child/young person and on their opportunities to be happy, healthy and safe. Assessments must make an analysis of what this means for them and whether they are suffering impairment or harm; and then make recommendations on what should happen next. This is a complex task. In this chapter, we will give you practical guidance on how to assess a child or young person's circumstances, manage risk and make safe decisions for them. However, before we look at how to do this, it's important to understand why we do this.

Why do we undertake assessments?

An important starting point in addressing this question is to consider what children tell us they want from a child protection system. According to the *Working Together to Safeguard Children and Young People* guidance (2018: 9), they want to feel protected 'against all forms of abuse and discrimination and the right to special protection and help if a refugee'. Our assessment should be focused on reducing the risk of abuse and harm experienced by the child and young person, as this can enhance safe decision-making and effective short- or long-term planning.

Furthermore, serious case reviews have shown the value of assessments that identify the risks and the likelihood of abuse as a means to prevent incidents of repeated abuse or even death of the child or young person. Overall, a good assessment can help to prevent delays in decision-making and reduce the potential of drift and a lack of direction in childcare planning (https://assets.publishing. service.gov.uk/government/uploads/system/uploads/attachment_data/file/197990 /DFE-RB092.pdf, accessed 25 May 2021).

What makes a good assessment?

A good assessment provides insight into the everyday experiences of the child and young person, contributing to clarity about the risks, both imminent and likely to face the child or young person within their home environment, and what, if anything, can mitigate these risks. An effective assessment will also capture what and who matters to the child or young person—in other words, the voice of the child can be heard and observed within the assessment.

Each assessment undertaken should have a clear goal and purpose in mind; ulti-mately, it must be focused on achieving a specific outcome for the child or young person, such as to stay with their current birth parent(s) with support or to identify an alternative caregiver on a temporary or permanent basis. Assessments tell us the child's story and represent a snapshot of a specific time in their life. A good assessment should therefore be ongoing and changing as the child and their experiences evolve. The *Working Together to Safeguard Children and Young People* guidance (2018: 24) states that an:

> Assessment should be a dynamic process, which analyses and responds to the changing nature and level of need and/or risk faced by the child from within and outside their family…

Now that we know why we do assessments and what the elements of a good assessment are, we will turn our attention to how to carry out an assessment.

How to undertake an assessment

The key tasks of an assessment are as follows:

- Gathering information
- Assessing the information gathered
- Making recommendations

Our Safeguarding Assessment and Decision-Making Tool, which was introduced in Chapter 1, provides a framework for you to use when undertaking assessments and guides you in reaching safe decisions for children and young people. We will link these three components of an assessment into our Safeguarding Assessment and Decision-Making Tool and show you how to use this tool in your safeguarding practice to undertake good assessments.

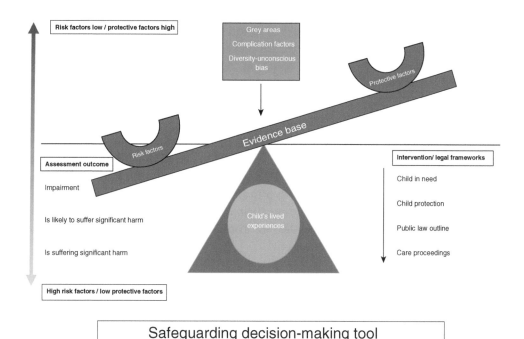

Safeguarding decision-making tool

Stage 1: Gathering information

The completion of a good assessment requires the health and social care professional to possess the relevant skills and knowledge to undertake this task confidently and effectively. Over recent years, local and national guidance have emerged to support the completion of high-quality assessments. The Department of Health and Social Care's Framework for the Assessment of Children in Need (2000) is a comprehensive and systematic approach to guide the collection of information to inform the analysis and decision-making stages of the assessment. The framework identifies three important areas of the child's life—each are interrelated and should be the basis of a good assessment as listed below:

- Child's developmental needs

- Parenting Capacity

- Family and Environmental Factors

As outlined in Figure 4.1, each domain below identifies key elements to be considered when assessing the level and quality of the relationships experienced by the child, the availability of support and resources from within the family and their local environment and the factors that might impede or stimulate the child's or young person's development. For example, the importance of an adequate diet, exercise and immunisation to support the healthy development of children and young people. In the domain of parenting capacity, factors such as the presence of emotional warmth and the importance of consistent and appropriate boundaries and guidance for behaviour management. The final domain of family and environmental factors requires closer examination of the influences impacting on the child's family. For example, how does structural factors such as housing status and tenure, income and employment impact on the child and their family. The factors identified in each domain will encourage a more in-depth review of the child's life story and in so doing promote a critical analysis of potential and actual risks within the completed assessment.

How does the information gathering stage of assessment fit in with our Safeguarding Assessment and Decision-Making Tool? Remember, in Chapter 1, we said the tool depicts a balance scale. The base of the scale is the DOH Assessment Framework (Figure 4.1), encouraging a practitioner to gather information about the child's lived experiences, including their individual needs, the parenting they receive and the environment they live in. In our tool, the base links to the information gathering stage of assessments.

Using Figure 4.1, let us look at a case study to consider how gathering information in each of these domains is important to assessment and risk analysis.

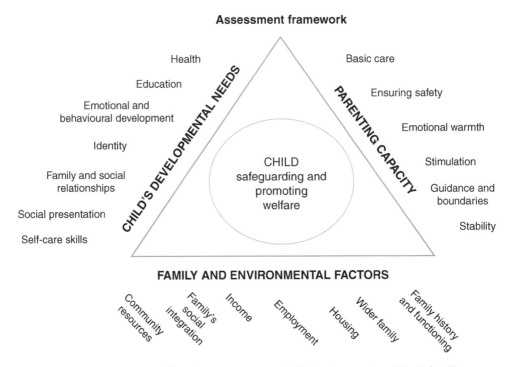

Figure 4.1   Framework for the assessment of children in need and their families (Department of Health, Department of Education and Employment, Home Office, 2000)

A referral is made from a midwife raising concerns for a mother who has just given birth to a baby girl. The mother is reported to be experiencing a severe episode of depression where she has no motivation, she is not looking after herself, she is eating poorly and has disrupted sleeping patterns. She is emotionally unresponsive and struggling to meet the care needs of her newborn baby.

Reflective questions

* *What about the child's individual needs, parenting she is receiving and environment she lives in must be considered?*

* *What factors will lower risks?*

* *What factors will increase risk?*

Comment

In this case study, the child is a baby. This increases the child's vulnerability. From our knowledge of child development, we know that as a newborn baby, she is fully reliant on adults to meet all her needs and keep her safe. The information we know about the mother's responses to the baby tells us she is providing an inadequate level of care. There is limited information about the wider family and community supports. Based on the information gathered so far, the risks of harm to the baby are high. If there is a presence of a supportive partner or a family member who can take on caring responsibilities and allow the baby to form secure attachments, this will significantly reduce the risks of harm to the child. If this is a single mother with no support network, the risks are increased. Is the mother linked to mental health services and is she engaging in treatment; how would that impact on risk assessment?

This case study shows how the domains are interrelated. Our safeguarding assessments must gather information from all three domains and in our analysis, we must consider whether the information from each domain increases or mitigates risk.

Stage 2: Assessing the information gathered

Assessments need to make recommendations that ensure safe outcomes for children and young people. To be able to do this, assessments need a good analysis. To analyse means to examine something closely and weigh up the meaning it holds. Analysis is where information that the professional has gathered is then sorted, weighted in terms of its significance and ultimately made sense of.

A safeguarding analysis should reflect on the information gathered and ask the following questions:

- What does this mean? What is the significance and impact of this on the child?
- Is this causing harm to the child?
- How can the risk be managed to keep the child safe?

In answering these questions, you need to consider what about the child's experiences places them at risk, and balance this against what about the child's experiences is protective and mitigates the risk. The Cambridge English Dictionary defines risk as 'the possibility of something bad happening'. In safeguarding, risk means the negative consequences and impact of the child or young person's experiences on them. This can be direct, for example, a non-accidental injury, sexually harmful behaviour, unkempt and unhygienic physical presentation, witnessing frightening adult behaviours, etc. Or it can be more subtle, for example, poor concentration and attainment at school or difficulties containing emotions and behaviours. By protective factors, we mean the things that reduce the risk to the child. This could be the child's age and ability to act protectively, a supportive family member or meaningful engagement with a service.

To make a good analysis, we must apply critical thinking skills in our approach to analysis. There are several examples available on how to undertake critical thinking. Here is an example by Rutter and Brown (2020) that you can use to guide you when considering a case.

Questions to develop descriptive reflection towards learning.

Description	Critical analysis	Evaluation	Learning
What did you do? What happened? What did you feel?	How did you do it? Why did you do it that way and not a different way? What was important and significant—why?	How far and in what ways were your goals met? What other factors were apparent?	So what does this mean for future practice and your values?

In our Safeguarding Assessment and Decision-Making Tool, the balance of the scale links to the analysis stage of assessments, where we are sorting and making sense of the information gathered and determining the significance of this for the child and young person, i.e. what is the likelihood of harm. The higher the number of risks and vulnerability factors identified, the higher the risk they are of suffering significant harm. The more protective factors there are, the better the risk can be managed. The following case study will show you how you can apply this in your safeguarding practice.

Consider the following case example and use our Safeguarding Assessment and Decision-Making Tool to make an analysis of the risks the child is exposed to.

CASE STUDY

You are a social worker, assigned to a new case. A referral has been made from A&E raising safeguarding concerns for a 10-year-old boy. The mother attended A&E with an overdose of prescribed medication; it is queried whether she took cocaine, and consumed a bottle of rum. The boy was having weekend contact with his father when the incident happened. He is now back in his mother's care. The information in the referral states that the mother was verbally abusive and aggressive to health care staff whilst in hospital. Support was required from hospital security. The mother has a strong belief her and her son have an autoimmune disease and was demanding a diagnosis. There are no symptoms observed to suggest either the mother or her son has an autoimmune disease. The mother self-discharged prior to review by mental health support teams. She is refusing to engage with children's services to complete the assessment and the boy has not been seen for his voice to be heard. You have received further information from the child's school, where the mother is sending several emails a day complaining that no professional is listening to her. The content and tone of the emails make them worried about her mental state.

Reflective questions

- *What analysis would you make about the child's experiences? Consider the following:*
  - *What are the risk factors?*
  - *What are the protective factors?*
  - *What is the level of risk to the child?*
  - *What framework should the case be managed under?*

Comment

In this case example, the risk and protective factors can be identified as follows:

Risk factors	Protective factors
The mother is presenting with unmanaged mental health needs, which are being observed by two different professional sources.	The child has contact with his father. No immediate concerns around the quality of this area are raised.
The mother has possibly used cocaine. Is this a regular habit or a maladaptive coping strategy?	

(Continued)

(Continued)

Risk factors	Protective factors
The mother has difficulties managing her emotions. From the descriptions in the referral, this is likely to be frightening and scary for a child.	
There is a query around the child and mother's actual health needs	
The mother is not engaging with Children's Services and Mental Health Services. This escalates risk. The child's voice is not heard	

In weighing up the information, you can see there are a higher number of risk factors, and the likelihood of the child suffering significant harm is high. A safety plan could include exploring and assessing the father's involvement with the child and the support he can offer. It is appropriate to hold a strategy discussion and for there to be multiagency information sharing and decision-making around whether the case should progress to a Child Protection Conference. The identified risks are likely to meet threshold to manage the case under child protection.

The use of tools in assessment

Munro (2008) defines risk assessment as 'the ability to predict future behaviours of parents, weigh up protective and risk factors. Assess the potential for change in a family, or with the parents'. This is the heart of our Assessment and Decision-Making Model. However, making sense of the information gathered and separating out what is a risk and what is protective can be challenging. The use of Assessment tools can help us to identify the significance of the information to the child. There are many effective tools that can be used; here are some suggestions (Table 4.1):

Table 4.1   Risk assessment models

Eileen Munro Risk Assessment Model (Munro, 2008)	Once we have gathered information, this model puts forward that risk and protective factors can be identified by asking the following questions: • What has been happening? • What is happening Now? • What might happen? • How likely is it? • How serious would it be?
Resilience Matrix http://www.ports mouthscb.org.uk/wp-content/uploads /Resilience-matrix.pdf	This model prompts you to look at factors that make the child resilient or vulnerable, and factors that make their environment protective or adverse. From your analysis and separating the information you have gained

	into the quadrants, you can make judgements as to whether the child is: • Vulnerable child in high adversity • Vulnerable child in a protective environment • Resilient children in high adversity • Resilient child in a protective environment (no risk)

REFLECTIVE QUESTIONS

• *What other assessment tools do you know of?*

• *How can you apply these tools, or others, in your safeguarding analysis and decision-making?*

In Chapter 1, we explored the four categories of harm. The safeguarding concerns we assess are whether the child is suffering or at risk of suffering, physical harm, sexual harm, emotional harm and neglect. The child may be experiencing one or more of these as a result of parental drug use, mental health, domestic abuse, learning difficulties or as a consequence of family cultural and religious beliefs such as in cases of Female Genital Mutilation, Forced Marriages and Spirit Possession. There are a range of assessment tools that are specific to certain risks factors such as these to aid our analysis of what this means for the child and whether it is causing them harm. Table 4.2 gives you some suggestions of further assessment tools for you to look up and use in your safeguarding risk assessment and analysis:

Table 4.2   Assessment tools

Domestic Abuse	**Safe Lives DASH Risk Assessment** https://www.cafcass.gov.uk/grown-ups/professionals/ciaf/resources-for-assessing-domestic-abuse/ **Barnardo's Domestic Violence Risk Identification Matrix** https://www.cafcass.gov.uk/grown-ups/professionals/ciaf/resources-for-assessing-domestic-abuse/
Sexual Harm	**Brook Sexual Behaviours Traffic Light Tool** https://www.enhertsccg.nhs.uk/sites/default/files/Sexual-Behaviours-Traffic-Light-Tool.pdf **Child Exploitation Screening Tool** https://www.cafcass.gov.uk/grown-ups/professionals/resources-for-professionals/

(Continued)

Table 4.2 (Continued)

Neglect	**Graded Care Profile** https://hertsscb.procedureonline.com/pdfs/app_3_gcp_summary_guid.pdf **Neglect Appraisal Tool** https://www.cafcass.gov.uk/grown-ups/professionals/resources-for-professionals/
Mental Health	**Mental Health thinking tool** https://www.cafcass.gov.uk/grown-ups/professionals/resources-for-professionals/ **Adult Wellbeing Tool**
Parental capacity to change	**Capacity to Change Tool** https://www.cafcass.gov.uk/grown-ups/professionals/resources-for-professionals/ **A 12-step process for assessing the risk of re-abuse to a child, parenting capacity and prospects of rehabilitation** https://www.cafcass.gov.uk/grown-ups/professionals/resources-for-professionals/

Now that we have pointed you to some tools, let's look at how one can be applied in practice.

CASE STUDY

You are the allocated social worker to a 15-year-old girl where there are concerns around child exploitation and child criminal exploitation. She regularly goes missing. She has been found by the police in multiple locations and with older men. On one occasion, police seized £30,000 of cocaine from the hotel room she was found in. Police checks show the men she has been found with are known for sex, violence and drug-related offences. She is out of education and known to the sexual health clinic. She has previously been subject to a child protection plan due to parental drug use and neglect. There is a pattern of missed appointments with support services.

- *Use one of the sexual harm tools identified in Table 4.2 to identify the risks to this fifteen-year-old girl.*

Comment

The assessment tool will help you to sort your information and assess what you know about the girl's experiences, against what you know about child sexual exploitation risk indicators. This will inform your assessment of the risk to the child. You will be able to make clear judgements on whether the child is vulnerable to exploitation, is being groomed or targeted or being actively exploited. Using tools in assessment will help you demonstrate defensible decision-making as it will help you explain how you reached your decision and the reasons why.

Stage 3: Managing risk and decision-making

A safeguarding analysis needs to make judgements on the level of risk the child is exposed to and make recommendations on what should happen next. Assessments must set out what the risk/risks are, whether they can be managed and what framework the case should be held open under to provide the identified support and intervention. 'Managing risk' means determining whether it is safe for the child to remain with their caregiver or in their current circumstance and what can be put in place, if anything, to reduce risks and make things safer.

Legal frameworks

From a statutory perspective, decisions need to be made on which framework a case should be managed under. The possible outcomes from an assessment are as follows:

- Case closure: where there are no risks identified

- Child in Need: where there are risks of impairment

- Child Protection: when the child is likely to suffer significant harm

- Public Law Outline: there is no change to the identified safeguarding concerns. This is the last opportunity to demonstrate change before going to court

- Care proceedings: the child or young person has suffered significant harm

The tipping scale imagery of our model will help you in making these judgements.

REFLECTIVE QUESTION

We have given you guidance on how to make an analysis. However, once you have sorted the information you have gathered into risk and protective factors, how do you make judgements on the level of risk and framework the case should be managed under?

- *What factors do you need to think about in determining the level of harm the child or young person is exposed to?*

We have developed a further tool to guide you in making these judgements. We will first explain the tool and then provide you with some case examples to support practice application.

RISK ANALYSIS AND MANAGEMENT TOOL

Aim of the Risk Analysis and Management Tool

This tool will support you in making professional judgements on the level of risk a child is exposed to, and whether the risk can be managed.

In safeguarding, there is no one size fits all and a careful analysis of the child and family's unique circumstances is required. This tool has been created to help you break down and understand risk in a practical way.

How to use the tool

The tool is designed with question prompts that are aimed at helping you determine the significance of the information you have gathered and what it means to the safety and well-being of a child. For each question there are indicators to support your thinking on whether the information you hold suggests the child is exposed to low risk, medium risk or high risk. These risk categories (low, medium, high) are formulated to resemble a traffic light system, and once you have worked through the questions, you will be able to make informed judgements on the level of risk the child is exposed to, and what framework the case be managed under.

The tool has a key:

Low Risk – a high number of low-risk indicators suggests the case is appropriate to be managed under Child In Need.

Medium Risk – a high number of medium-risk indicators suggests the case should be managed under Child Protection.

High Risk – a high number of high-risk indicators suggests the case is appropriate to be managed under PLO/Care proceedings.

This tool should not replace discussions with your line manager about risk. Rather, it is aimed to support your decision-making of risk.

This tool can be used throughout the life of a case to assess changes in risk.

	Low risk	Medium risk	High risk
What is the current risk? What is happening to the child?	☐ Emerging/identified needs	☐ The child is likely to experience harm if there is no change to circumstances/experiences	☐ The child is experiencing actual harm (i.e. direct non-accidental injury; sexual assault; health need as a result of neglect; low mood)
Are there multiple risk factors? The higher the number of risk factors, the higher the risk.	☐ 1–2 risk factors	☐ 3–4 risk factors	☐ 4 or more risk factors
Is there past harm? Have similar incidents occurred in the past? When? How often? Was support and intervention put in place? Is there a pattern of harmful behaviour?	☐ First incident	☐ Incidents have happened before; there have been short periods of change/managing; there are questions around the ability to sustain change	☐ Repeat incidents of worrying/harmful behaviours
How is risk perceived by other professionals? What is their assessment of risk, i.e. have police made a charge? What is the view of experts such as mental health professional/drugs and alcohol worker, etc.	☐ Low	☐ Moderate	☐ High
How many professionals have the same concern?	☐ 1–2 professionals	☐ 3–4 professionals	☐ 4 or more professionals
Age of child?	☐ 10+ have increased understanding and more	☐ 5–10	☐ 0–5 years

(Continued)

75

RISK ANALYSIS AND MANAGEMENT TOOL *continued*

What is the child's developmental stage and are they able to act protectively?	likely to use protective behaviours ☐	Starting to develop skills to protect/speak up for themselves ☐	Are most vulnerable and most dependent on safe and reliable care giving ☐
Needs of the child? Does the child have any additional health needs that require support or which makes them more vulnerable to exposed risk?	No additional health needs ☐	Low care and support needs ☐	High support and dependency needs ☐
What is the parental insight into risk? Do they accept concerns? Is there motivation to change?	Parents accept concerns and are willing to engage with identified services ☐	Parents deciding on the need to change and any change needs to be tested out ☐	Parents do not have any insight; they do not see their actions as harmful or a need to change ☐
Is the harm caused intentional or unintentional? Is the harm impacted by a parental need or a choice?	Harm is unintentional, caused by a parental need, i.e. physical need from a health condition; learning disability. Issues can be easily addressed and supported ☐	Harm is caused by a situation that is influenced by factors outside of parental control, i.e. acute psychosis, or not having the resources to leave a domestically abusive situation. Are parents able to make changes/take control of the situation to making things better? Can this happen in the child's timescales? ☐	Parent actively chooses to engage in risky behaviours and fails to prioritise the needs of a child ☐
What is the parent's experience of being parented? What is their model of parenting to draw on?	Good parenting; no disruption to care giving ☐	Experienced social work intervention ☐	Disruption to care giving, experienced time in care ☐

	Low risk Indicators	Medium Risk Indicators	High risk Indicators
Is there family/friends support available? What is the quality of family relationships? Are they readily available to offer support? Do they show insight into the risks and have the capacity to act protectively? Is the child familiar to them? Do they present with any risk factors?	Family/friends available who can provide tangible support ☐ / Show insight into the risks ☐ / Do not present with risk factors ☐ / Child knows them well	Family/friends are not local to provide practical support ☐ / Show some insight into concerns, but needs further exploring/assessment! ☐ / Present with some risk factors/can these be managed? ☐ / Child knows of them	Fractious/poor quality relationships ☐ / No insight into safeguarding concerns ☐ / Present with high risk factors ☐ / Child is unfamiliar to them
What support/interventions are available that could make the circumstances safer? Is the support appropriate to identified need? Is the parent willing to engage with it? Funding?	Courses/support are readily available, and parents are motivated to engage with them ☐	Interventions available but there is a delay to starting the course, i.e. the course is not available; it clashes with work commitments; there is no funding; parents does not agree to support ☐	There is no support and unwillingness of parent to engage in any support ☐
Are there any laws that must be considered? i.e. around physical chastisement/home schooling, etc.? Are parental behaviours within these boundaries?	Behaviour within boundaries ☐	Borderline behaviours ☐	Behaviour breaks the law ☐
Total number	Low risk Indicators	Medium Risk Indicators	High risk Indicators
What is your assessment of the level of risk the child is exposed to?			
What can mitigate the risk, and are there indicators to suggest the child can be safe in the community?			

Now use the Risk Analysis and Management Tool to make a judgement on risk for the following two case examples:

CASE STUDY

Adrian is a thirteen-year-old boy. He has a diagnosis of hypermobility and chronic fatigue syndrome. There was a professionals meeting and the following concerns have been raised in a referral to social care.

- *Adrian is not being allowed to access education as mother does not wish for him to attend the school that has been recommended to him via the tribunal process. He is being homeschooled in the interim.*

- *Adrian spends all day accessing the Internet without supervision and could be accessing inappropriate websites that leave him vulnerable to abuse.*

- *Adrian is not able to express what he would like to achieve. When he expressed to the physiotherapist that he would like to go out and go to school, mother subsequently made a complaint and withdrew him from the service.*

Information gathered:

- *There is a good level of basic care being provided to Adrian.*

- *There is no previous contact with children's services.*

- *The physiotherapist reports that the impact of not accessing physio is, whether the young person is getting input for less pain, his daily living skills are improving and building up to accessing school.*

- *The mother reports that she is accessing private physio.*

- *The child told you about activities he does throughout the day.*

Reflective questions

- *What judgements would you make about risk?*

- *What framework should the case be managed under?*

Comment

The risk is moderate and could be managed under child in need. Home education is not illegal. There are no concerns being raised that the level of learning being provided is inadequate. The concerns around internet use are not a factual concern and could be addressed through protective behaviours including e-safety. Mother is accessing private physiotherapy to meet Adrian's needs. There are identified needs that can be managed safely with appropriate resources.

CASE STUDY

You are completing an assessment on the family. The child, Ben, is four years old. Mother is pregnant with her second child (Unborn Baby). The children have different fathers and mother is not currently in a relationship. The following information has been gathered:

- *Mother has a history of being in relationships that are domestically abusive. The children's fathers each have police records for violence and drug-related offences.*

- *Mother has a diagnosis of an emotionally unstable personality disorder. She makes impulsive decisions and seeks out risky sexual relationships. She admits to having sex with a man whilst Ben was in the same room.*

- *A change in Ben's behaviours has been observed since this incident. He is wetting himself and presenting as withdrawn at the nursery.*

- *Mother has experienced two episodes in care as a child, being exposed to domestic abuse in her own parent's relationship.*

- *Mother states she is receiving support from her own mother (maternal grandmother); but you have observed tension in this relationship which can impact on mother's engagement with Children's services.*

- *Mother is honest with professionals about her behaviours, and admits she is struggling to cope.*

Reflective questions

- *What do you assess the level of risk to be?*

- *What, if any, support can be put in place to make the circumstances safe for the children?*

Comment

Using the tool, you will see there are many indicators to suggest the risk is 'high risks' and it is not safe for the children to remain in the mother's care. The risks should be discussed with your line manager and conversations started around whether there is threshold to initiate care proceedings. It is possible for care support to be put in place, but this too would require many hours per day, and it would need to be balanced whether this is proportionate to 'the right for family life'?

Evidenced-based decision-making

Evidence-based decision-making became integral to safeguarding following Professor Eileen Munro's report on her review of the child protection process (Munro, 2011). It means that when making an analysis and reaching decisions for children and young people, we need to think about what information is available to support the professional judgements that are being made about the child's lived experiences. Safeguarding concerns need to be substantiated. The concerns raised need to be corroborated and verified against other sources of information.

ACTIVITY **4.1**

- *Where can we get information from to ensure our analysis and decision-making is evidenced based?*

The evidence in our assessments can come from a range of sources including:

- Communication with the child, mother and father. What have they told us about their experiences.

- Your professional observations of the child or young person.

- Feedback from other professionals including:

    - GP reports and reports from other health professionals such as mental health.

    - Police reports.

    - Welfare reports from schools/education authorities.

    - Other universal and targeted services involved in the family.

To help us understand the importance of an evidence base in assessments, let's link this to our Assessment and Decision-Making Tool. The balance, or rather the beam which holds the weight of the risk and protective factors and tips accordingly, needs to be solid to hold this weight. Therefore, in our assessment, we need to be clear and certain why we are saying what we say and be able to refer to where the supporting information comes from.

The following case study will develop your thinking around this point.

You receive a referral from a primary school. The designated safeguarding lead is making a referral for James who is eight years old. She is concerned that his parents are often late to fetch him from school, and when they collect him, they appear to be under the influence of substances. James often falls asleep in class. The case progresses to an assessment.

Reflective question

What information do you need to gather and from where to make an evidenced-based analysis about the risks to James' safety and well-being?

Comment

In this example of James, feedback about James' experiences and the risks he is exposed to can be gathered by making the following enquiries.

- Complete direct work with James: what does he tell you about his lived experiences?

- Interview parents: what is their substance use? Do they accept it? Do they show insight into how it is impacting on James?

- GP check: this will share information about parental health, including any intervention for substance misuse.

- Police check: this will identify any offences, including drug-related offences.

- School Welfare report information on James' progress at school: this will help us understand the impact of any parental drug use.

- Check with Drug and Alcohol Support services: are the family previously or currently known? What is their engagement?

The information gathered from these sources will form the evidence base for your assessment and decision-making.

When considering the feedback from partner agencies, it is important to not only get the facts, for example, mother attended three appointments at a drug and alcohol supports service, but also gather a depth of information to enable us to understand what this means for the safety and well-being of a child. Is there meaningful engagement with services? How do we know this? What does this mean for the ongoing risk to the child?

Defensible decision-making

Decisions and recommendations that we make in our assessments must be defensible. Defensible decision-making shows your working out and what you took account of when reaching your decisions; this includes the following:

1. Hypothesis that can be tested

2. Recordings that show 'working out'

3. Gathering of information from all sources

4. Research and theory clearly recorded to support findings

5. Legislative basis for intervention clear and stated

6. Any decisions that require consultation and authorisation documented and signed

7. Policy and processes of the organisation known and adhered to

8. Information sharing clearly recorded and signed by other parties including the family and child.

(*Source:* Northamptonshire Children's Social Care Services, 2013)

It is important to be clear about what you are recommending, the reasons for it and the evidence base which supports this. Drawing on theory, research and assessment tools supports defensible decision-making. We look at how we can apply this later in this chapter.

Shared decision-making

The decisions social care professionals make directly impact on a child and are far-reaching. This would be an immense responsibility on any one professional, and it is important to remember that all decision-making is shared.

The law provides for this at all levels of intervention with children and families:

*   All assessments are approved by a manager who shares in decision-making.

*   Under the Child in Need framework, decisions about the changes that need to be achieved to promote a child's well-being are jointly agreed and reviewed by the members of the Child in Need plan. If there is a change, this needs to be agreed by the members.

*   The Children Act 1989 gives clear guidance on Child Protection procedures. For example, at a minimum, representatives from the social care and police should participate in a strategy discussion where decisions are made whether a case should progress to a Child Protection Conference. A Child Protection Conference must be quorate for it to proceed. This means there has to be a minimum of

four different professionals to allow for joint decision-making. The members of the core group review and monitor progress of the child protection plan.

- Even within care proceedings, whilst a judge ultimately makes a final decision, he is assisted to make the decision by considering written and oral evidence from Local Authority, parents, experts and the appointed guardian.

Report writing

What is a report?

An assessment is formally recorded as a written document, a report. This is shared with the child (where appropriate), the parents and sometimes professionals. Reports will be required for different forums such as Child in Need Reviews, Child Protection Conferences, Court Reports and Child Looked after Reviews, as well as reports when requesting services and interventions.

What makes a good report?

This chapter has discussed elements of a good assessment including the importance of information gathering, evidence-based analysis and defensible decision-making. These should come through in the written record of the assessment.

Just like an assessment, a good report should do the following:

- Describe what is going on for the child and young person.
- Be evidenced based.
- Have a strong analysis.
- Acknowledge gaps in information and set out how these impact on decision-making.
- Make clear recommendations on the level of harm the child is exposed to and what should happen next.

The written record should use simple, jargon-free language that is accessible to all readers.

Reflecting on what you have learned from this chapter, and returning to the example of James in the previous case study, let's think about how you can apply these principles of assessment and report writing into safeguarding practice.

Compare the following two examples of report writing.

Report 1:

I am worried that James' parents use drugs. This is impacting on his learning at school. He will be at risk of harm if no change is made. The case should progress to a child protection conference.

- What is missing in this report?

- How can this assessment be improved?

Now consider Report 2:

CASE STUDY

I am concerned that James is at risk of suffering harm due to parental drug use. Research tells us that parental drug use can lead to neglect of a child's needs as when under the influence of substances, a parent can be unaware or unresponsive to a child's needs. This is James lived experience. James told me that at home, 'his parents are always drinking wine' and that 'he gets to do what he wants'. I completed a home visit and observed the bin was overflowing with empty alcohol bottles and that there was no emotional warmth in the exchanges between James and his mother. I further note the concerns from the primary school that James is not collected on time. It is clear James' needs are being neglected which are impacting on his self-confidence and learning opportunities at school, and his supervision at home.

Feedback from the police shows that mother was arrested for possession of class A drugs two months ago, and feedback from the GP tell us that she has attended A&E on two occasions for overdoses. This suggests there are long-standing issues with alcohol and illicit substances, and these are ongoing and live risks for James.

Mother has recently started engaging with drug support services, who have confirmed mother's attendance at the last three support sessions. Her last drug and alcohol screening was clear, indicating she had not used substances in the last week. The school have updated that since the referral has been made, James has been collected on time. This is important for James' sense of belonging and mother must be encouraged to keep this up. It is a positive that mother is expressing a motivation to change; however, the concerns are long-standing and she will need to demonstrate that she can remain abstinent and prioritise James' needs over a sustained period. James is likely to have poor outcomes if changes to his experiences are not made. It is my assessment that James is likely to suffer significant harm, and the case should progress to a child protection conference. This will allow the necessary monitoring of James' safety whilst services are provided to the family to support them in achieving changes and making things better for James.

In Report 2, the voice of the child is heard, and the analysis draws on an evidence base from research, the social worker's observations and feedback from multiple professionals. It further considers parental insight/motivation and identifies strengths. The decision to progress to a child protection conference is defensible because it sets out the evidence base for the concerns, the impact it is having on the child and why the decisions are being made. Report 1 lacked all these key elements of a report.

Sharing the report

The assessment and recommendations when completed should be shared with the young person and their family. The format of the report should be clear and easily accessible to the child and young person. Providing the report to the young person is not enough; adequate time is essential for families to read and ask questions or contest the information in the assessment.

Working to Safeguard Children and Young People guidance states that:

> *It is important that the impact of what is happening to a child is clearly identified and that information is gathered, recorded and checked systematically, and discussed with the child and their parents/carers where appropriate.*
>
> *(2018: 24)*

Let's think about these principles of report sharing in the following reflective questions.

REFLECTIVE QUESTIONS

- *When sharing a report, how can you ensure the family or child has the opportunity to read the information and request any changes?*

- *How can you share information to take into account the literacy and language needs of the reader? For example, if you have a 15-year-old with autism, how might you share the recommendations?*

Comment

When sharing the report, it is good practice to ensure the child and family receive the report in time and have an opportunity to fully considered it before any meeting. You should make time to discuss the report with the child and family and give them the opportunity to respond to the recommendations. This forms part of your ongoing assessment of parents' acceptance of concerns and motivation to change. It is good practice guidelines to be honest with families at the start of the process about the difference between fact and professional opinion, and the changes that can and cannot be made to an assessment/report.

Chapter 2 looked at the factors to consider when communicating with children and young people. These should be applied when deciding whether a full report is shared with the child, or whether verbal feedback is enough. It's important to tell the child about the recommendations being made, and what they will mean for them going forward, and to seek their views on how they feel about this.

Diversity and equality in assessments

At the beginning of the chapter, we talked about the assessment including three key tasks:

- Gathering information

- Assessing the information gathered

- Making recommendations

Our practice when undertaking the above tasks should promote equality and diversity for the child and their family. Reflect on the following diversity and equality issues which you may come across. What measures can be taken to promote these diversity needs? Discuss, if necessary, with your line manager.

We must always ensure that the child/young person and family can actively engage in the process and have a fair assessment.

You are doing an assessment on a family where the child is deaf and attends a school for children who are hard of hearing	You are undertaking an assessment of a parent with suspected learning difficulties.	Can a family request changes to the report to reflect their diversity needs?
Who should you use to interpret, a trusted member from the school or an independent interpreter? What other factors should be considered when making this decision?	What adjustments do you need to make in your language, communication techniques and length of interviews? Should the parent be offered the support of an advocate?	Are the changes requested an incorrect fact or a difference between family/ professional opinion? How can you ensure the information in the assessment appropriately addresses the diversity needs of the child and family?

Assessments and a remote way of working

When we undertake assessments, we are dealing with sensitive information. In the information gathering stage, we are receiving information about a child and family from themselves and partner agencies, we are also writing a report, a written record of the assessment setting out what is going well for them and what we are worried about. Therefore, when thinking about assessments and a remote way of working pertinent to this, how do we manage information safely?

REFLECTIVE QUESTIONS

- *Can you share a report electronically with a parent?*
- *Can you receive a report electronically from a partner agency?*

Comment

The answer is yes; however, we need to ensure the information is being sent securely, the parent has access to the technology to receive the report and that the email address is verified before sending the information.

Chapter summary

This chapter has covered the following:

- The key stages of an assessment: gathering information, assessing the information and making recommendations.
- How to apply Our Assessment and Decision-Making Tool and Risk Analysis and Management Tool.
- Case studies and assessment tools to support your assessment, decision-making and critical thinking skills.
- Examples of 'good' and 'bad' report writing.
- Diversity and equality and remote working issues in social work practice.

YOUR LEARNING JOURNEY

This chapter has focused on assessment, managing risk and decision-making. We have introduced you to our own Assessment and Decision-Making Tool and Risk Analysis and Management Tool, providing a framework for you to undertake assessments. We have also suggested a range of tools for you to use in your analyses. Stop and Think:

- *From reading this chapter, what have you learned about assessment, managing risk and decision-making?*
- *How will you apply this in your practice?*
- *Use two of the tools discussed in the chapter in your risk assessments. Research and use another assessment tool.*
- *Using one of the case studies in this book, write a report.*

Chapter 5

Interventions: achieving good outcomes

Chapter objectives

This chapter seeks to answer these questions:

- What are interventions?

- What is an effective approach to Interventions?

- What makes a good intervention plan?

- Whose responsibility is it to monitor interventions?

- How will we know good outcomes are achieved?

- What if we are not achieving good outcomes?

Introduction

Interventions are the support, strategies or plans designed to bring about change. The aim of the intervention is to make things better and safer for children and young people. As outlined in Chapter 4, an assessment weighs up the risks and protective factors for a child to identify the key concerns, considers the behaviours or environment that requires change and makes recommendations on how to address these issues to achieve positive outcomes for the child. What happens after the assessment stage matters most to the child, and as Teater (2012: 01) reminds us, 'a key element of the social work process is the selection of the intervention methods'. After all, it is futile to identify what needs to change, or be different, and then do nothing to support or enable this.

The range of intervention methods that can inform social work practice are broadly speaking based upon theories that are sociological or psychological. A social work intervention must set out the type of tools, activities, courses and actions to be used, in social work practice with the child/young person and their family.

The key tasks of the social worker in providing interventions are as follows:

- formulating the intervention plan,

- monitoring the progress of the intervention plan,

- assessing/reassessing if the situation is improving for the child and young person, and whether they are happier and safer,

- deciding when interventions should end, or alternative support should be provided, or the case should escalate if there is no progress to the plan.

This chapter looks at how to do this. We will look at what factors should be considered when formulating and providing interventions, and how we can ensure positive change is achieved for children and young people.

Formulating an intervention plan

When formulating an intervention plan you need to think about both your approach and the factors which influence what goes into an intervention plan.

What is an effective approach to interventions?

In safeguarding practice, we have statutory responsibilities to keep children safe, and our assessments must identify what is working well for the family (the strengths) and what is not working well for the family (the risks). When families reach the attention of social workers, there will be more risks factors identified, and families will respond to assessments in different ways. For example, they may accept and show insight into the risks, or they may feel heavily criticised and shut off, or disengage. The challenge social workers have is to maintain a working relationship with families after an assessment and support the families to engage with identified interventions. Therefore, developing and implementing an effective intervention plan will draw on knowledge, skills, and the ability to build and maintain productive working relationships with children and their families. As Teater (2012: 01) comments:

> *Implementing the intervention requires skills in communication ....as well as critical reflection & analysis in order to evaluate the interventions effectiveness (whether through formal or informal evaluative methods).*

Take time to think about the following reflective questions to develop your thinking on how to approach interventions with children and families.

REFLECTIVE QUESTION

- *How would you feel when the things you are doing wrong are highlighted to you?*

- *What factors would help you engage in changing?*

- *How can you continue building a working relationship with children and families that supports and motivates them to engage with interventions?*

When considering social work intervention our approach should be grounded in a strengths-based approach to social work practice (Winnicott, 1965). According to this approach, the individual (child) is at the centre of the intervention and we seek to recognise the strengths of the child/young person and their family. When planning an intervention, the child and their family will have strengths and resources already around them that can be drawn upon and developed as part of the intervention stage. The intervention requires the social worker to not only see and respond to the risks and support families to achieve safer parenting practices but also illuminate the potential of families too.

Collaborating with the family and hearing the voice of the young person or child is critical to adopting a strengths-based approach to interventions. The strengths-based approach supports the development of plans that are realistic, achievable and promotes the concept of 'good enough parenting'. Good enough parenting suggests that the goal is not perfectionism but instead should focus on what is necessary to enable a child to grow and thrive in their home environment (Winnicott, 1965). More recently the work of Kellett and Apps (2009) offers insight into four factors that might demonstrate good enough parenting:

- Meeting the child's health and developmental needs

- Putting the child first

- Providing routine and consistent care

- Parental acknowledgement and engagement with support services (2009: 27).

Choate and Engstrom (2014) would suggest that there must be an element of caution applied to using the term 'good enough parenting', as 'It appears to be done without any formal, cohesive or commonly accepted definition or under-standing about what it fully means' (2014: 13).

That said, a strengths-based approach applied to social work interventions rec-ognises the importance of the social workers' reflective skills, such as empathy and affirming to reveal and build on the existing strengths in the family. The devel-opment of effective intervention will, therefore, also be dependent on the avail-ability of effective reflective supervision opportunities for the social worker practitioner at work.

What factors need to be considered when providing interventions?

Interventions can be observed at differing levels in the intervention stage. The Ecological model, developed by Urie Bronfenbrenner (1979), provides a helpful framework for understanding what social work interventions are and how they occur at the various levels. As outlined in Figure 5.1, the Ecological approach consists of three main levels that can be applied to social work practice.

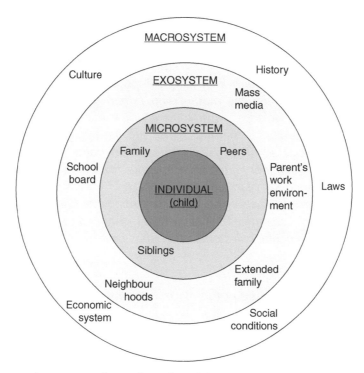

Figure 5.1   The Ecological model (Bronfenbrenner, 1979)

Micro—The focus is on direct work with children and families.

Meso—The focus is on the context surrounding the individual, such as their family and caregivers.

Macro—The focus is on the wider socio-economic and political systems to understand why people have certain experiences beyond the individual and family.

Interventions should seek to address the concerns at the micro, meso and macro level. To understand this better, let us turn back to what we said in Chapter 4.

Chapter 4 identified the importance of the Assessment Framework Triangle when carrying out assessments. To make a good and comprehensive assessment of the child's day-to-day experiences, we need to look at the child, parental and environmental factors. Therefore, to provide effective interventions, we must hold on to what we know and have assessed about these factors and look at what support can be provided to the child, to the parents/the caregiving relationships and wider environmental supports to make things better and safer for the child and young person. The following case example will show you how to apply this when formulating an intervention plan and providing interventions.

CASE STUDY

An assessment has been completed and decisions made for the case to be managed under Child in Need. The family is at risk of eviction due to rent arrears. This is causing arguments between the mother and father which have escalated into incidents of domestic violence. Mostly there are verbal arguments which can become loud, but emotionally harmful words are used by each parent. On two occasions this has escalated into physical attacks where police have been called. The mother has sustained a minor injury, scratch marks, from the father. There are two children at home aged six years and two years. It is unclear whether they have witnessed the arguments. The six-year-old is presenting as withdrawn at school. The one-year health check assessment by health visitor identified the youngest child was not reaching developmental milestones. There has been no further follow-up.

Reflective question

- *What interventions can be put in place at the micro, meso and macro level? Write these down.*

Comment

What interventions did you come up with? Some suggestions on the possible interventions that could be provided at the micro, meso and macro level in this case study are included in Table 5.1.

Table 5.1   Interventions at micro, meso and macro level

Micro (Interventions for the child)	• Counselling should be provided to the six-year-old child to explore her wishes and feelings. Can the school provide this? What support could the school nurse provide? Is a referral to Step 2 or CAMHS required? • 1-year-old child: what milestones are not being met? Do health services need to provide further support such as physiotherapy, or Speech and Language Therapy?
Meso (Interventions for the parents)	• Refer parents to participate in domestic abuse intervention programmes, such as The Freedom Program, Triple R. • Does a referral for their mental well-being need to be made?
Macro (Interventions for the wider environmental factors)	• Refer to Money Advice Unit, for support with budgeting etc. • Is intervention/mediation required with Housing? • Referral to Citizen Advice Unit (is employment an issue?) • Support to access food bank?

Social workers are based in a diverse range of practice settings, such as schools, hospitals and local authority children and family's teams and family support services. The interventions applied in social work practice will be influenced by a number of factors, such as the issues identified that require change, the setting and context that surrounds the child/young person, the social workers' knowledge and skills about the types of interventions available and the availability of interventions; for example, are interventions accessible and is there funding available for them.

What makes a good intervention plan?

Interventions need to be timely, and prevent drift and delay for the child. This means that once interventions are identified, they must be implemented, monitored and reviewed, to ensure they are making a positive difference for the child and young person.

Below are some factors that make a good intervention plan:

- Clear outcomes that show what should be achieved during the intervention stage.

- Evidence of a strengths-based approach throughout.

- Explains clearly who is responsible and how for the intervention.

- Measures that evaluate the effectiveness of the plan (views of the child, reports from other professionals, e.g. GP/consultant/Family contact worker).

- The voice of the child is demonstrated by hearing and explaining how the child has experienced the intervention.

- The interventions are achievable and realistic.

- Options are available if the intervention plan is not progressing as planned.

Now that you know what makes a good intervention plan, let's have a go at writing one.

ACTIVITY **5.1**

The previous case study gave a scenario and asked you to come up with interventions/support services that could be provided at a micro, meso and macro level. Using the interventions that you identified, write an intervention plan which fully details the elements of a good intervention plan.

To support you in this task, we have devised some question prompts for you to use when for formulating intervention plans in your safeguarding practice. These are based on Hertfordshire Children's Services care plan templates, as well as

(Continued)

additional questions of our own. Using these questions as a guide will ensure your intervention plans are focused and effective.

- What are we worried about? *This identifies the concerns and breaks down the issues that need addressing at the micro, meso and macro levels.*

- What are we doing about it? *We must set out clearly what support is being put in place to improve things for the child. This requires you to know:*

- What services or resources are available to address the identified risk? *You will need to have knowledge of resources in your area and need to think about when they are likely to available. For example, when is the start date of any intervention, or is there a waiting list? Is it free or does funding need to be secured? What can be put in place until the resource is available? Out of the available resources, what is the best assessed intervention for the family?*

- Who needs to be part of the intervention plan?

- What will they be doing and what will they be responsible for? *There should be clear accountability to ensure the intervention is implemented.*

- By when should it be done? *All actions need to be set to a timescale. This is important as it prevents drift and delay for the child and allows interventions to be provided timely.*

- How will we know it is achieved? *There should be a clear idea of what interventions we are aiming for.*

- What will happen if interventions are not achieved? *There should be a statement setting out what will happen if there is non-engagement with the intervention plan. That is, the case will escalate to child protection, or the local authority will seek legal advice.*

- What is the parallel plan? *What if your intervention plan is not progressing or the identified resources are not available?*

Using these prompts, finish the intervention plan for the case study. We have completed the first action of the intervention plan to start you off.

What are we worried about?	What are we doing about it?	Who is responsible for doing it?	By when should it be done?	How will we know it is achieved?
Domestic abuse: police have been called for arguments	Both parents to attend a domestic abuse course	Social worker to make referral to the domestic abuse change programme; parents to	Referral to be made by XXXX for parents to start the course on XXXX. The	There are no further police calls-outs or reports of physical attacks.

What are we worried about?	What are we doing about it?	Who is responsible for doing it?	By when should it be done?	How will we know it is achieved?
between parents		attend weekly sessions	course will run for eight weeks	Improvements to the child's emotional presentation are observed

Comment

We hope that with the question prompts and example, you were able to write an intervention plan that was accessible for the family, with clear actions on what they need to do to achieve change, how they will be supported to do this, by when they need to demonstrate change, and how we will know change is achieved. There is an emphasis on plans being SMART: Specific, Measurable, Achievable, Realistic and Timely.

What happens if a resource is not readily available, or during the monitoring of the intervention plan (which is discussed next) it is identified an action is not being met? When devising our interventions plans, it is important to **parallel plan**. This is to have a Plan B when Plan A fails. In social work practice, the child's welfare must be at the forefront of our thinking and we must have a plan for the best-case scenario and worst-case scenario. The plans must run side by side so that there is no delay for the child.

> **REFLECTIVE QUESTION**
>
> *Again, using the above case study, what would be your parallel plan if:*
>
> - Scenario 1: *A domestic abuse programme was not due to start until three months?*
>
> - Scenario 2: *The number of arguments, injuries to the mother became more serious, and police call-outs increased?*

Comment

In Scenario 1, you would need to discuss with your manager what could be put in place to bridge the gap, such as the social worker carrying out some individual sessions or thinking creatively about where else the intervention could be provided.

In Scenario 2, you will need to discuss the increasing risks with your manager and whether the case needs to escalate to be managed under a more protective framework, and whether it is safe for the child to remain at home. The parallel plan should form part of your risk statement in your intervention plan so parents are aware what could happen if change is not achieved.

Monitoring the progress of interventions

Once interventions are identified, we need to monitor and review the progress of them.

Who is responsible for implementing and monitoring interventions?

Safeguarding is everybody's responsibility, and the law sets out a multiagency approach to safeguarding and improving outcomes for children and young people. When concerns for a child's safety and well-being are raised, either under S17 (Child In Need) or S47 (Child Protection) of the Children Act 1989, a team automatically forms around a child to share information on what is known about the child and to enable assessments to be completed and judgements on risk to be made. This team will comprise different professionals from a range of agencies, and at the core is social care, police, health and education. Any other agency/agencies the child is accessing contribute too. The assessment will identify which professionals are playing an active role with the child and need to continue to be involved with the child. The interventions, the identified actions to improve outcomes for a child, should be jointly agreed between those professionals recognised as playing an active role with the child and family. This is usually agreed at the first review meeting.

The social worker has lead responsibilities in overseeing and monitoring the intervention plan for the child/young person, and these responsibilities may include tasks such as organising regular meetings, writing up meeting outcomes and ongoing risk assessment.

A multiagency approach to safeguarding, including interventions, means there is shared accountability between the child, family and involved professionals to achieve the set outcomes/interventions on the child's plan. Families and professionals have responsibilities to do the following:

- Provide the support/service assigned to them.
- Share information on engagement, progress of the support and the impact it is having on the child.

- Consider whether interventions are effective or whether alternative interventions are necessary.

- Feedback on any further identified risks and protective factors.

How are interventions monitored?

The child's care plan is reviewed through regular meetings. This can be under different frameworks such as Child in Need meetings, Core Group meetings (when a child is subject to a child protection plan) or Children Looked After Review, depending on the identified level of risk.

The Children Act 1989 sets out the statutory frequency of these meetings as follows:

- Child in Need: 6 times weekly

- Child Protection: 4–6 times weekly

- Child Looked After: First review within 21 days of becoming looked after, then every 3–6 months.

The purpose of care plan review meetings is to consider each identified action, to evaluate if there has been engagement from the family, and to identify how the interventions are making a difference for the child and reducing risk. Some questions for consideration might include the following:

- Has the outcome been achieved? How do we know this?

- Is this service still needed?

- Is further support required?

For a review meeting to be effective, attendance and contributions of the child, family and involved professionals are necessary. Within these meeting, those in attendance should provide updates on what's working well for the child, what's still a worry or concern and what are the remaining grey areas, for example, the uncertainties, and missing information.

Examples of feedback at a review meeting:

Feedback from a partner agency providing a parenting course might be:

Example A: 'The course started on 02.01.2021, the mother and father attend the parenting programme weekly, they ask relevant questions and reflect on the course content and come back the following week to give examples of how they have used something which they learned'.

Or, it could be,

Example B: 'they have been offered 7 sessions; they have only attended 2, they appear distracted and not to be taking anything onboard'.

If there are incidents or further safeguarding concerns outside of the review meetings, these should be reported to the social worker immediately, and the issues must not wait to be reported at the next review meeting. The child's immediate safety must always be prioritised.

Do children attend reviews meetings?

Children are at the centre of the plan. A child's attendance at a review meeting should be judged on their age and level of understanding. In reality, often it is inappropriate for a child to attend the full duration of review meeting as often these are emotionally charged, the content is difficult and it can be overwhelming if there are high numbers of professionals. If it is not appropriate for a child to attend, consider whether a child can attend for ten minutes at the beginning or end; and if not, their views should be obtained before the meeting to be shared within the meeting. Their views can be captured in writing, by pictures or recordings from visits.

PRACTICE TIPS FOR CARRYING OUT A REVIEW MEETING

- *Remember the basics: at the start of the meeting:*
    - *Introduce the attendees and record who is attending the meeting, what their involvement is with the child and their contact details.*
    - *Explain the purpose of the meeting.*
    - *Set out the expectations and boundaries of the meeting (i.e. confidentiality, time constraints, how to deal with disagreements and challenges).*
- *Have copies of the agenda for meeting attendees. It is natural for social workers to develop different styles for chairing meetings, but it is helpful to take a methodological approach, and to address each action, one at a time, and talk about what progress has been made and what impact it has had on the child or young person and family.*
- *Think about how long the meeting should go on for? Meetings can often be intense for families and an average time limit of 45–90 minutes is sensible. This considers parents' concentration and needs and respects the attendees' time. It is okay to take breaks during the meeting if needed.*
- *Remain focused on the purpose of the meeting. Often there are discussions that are not relevant to the meeting; be firm and clear in stating they are important, but there is a different setting to have them.*
- *At the end of the meeting summarise the key discussions and confirm the ongoing and new actions and outcomes.*
- *Set dates to actions. By when must the action be achieved? This prevents drift and delay for the child.*

- *Set a date for the next meeting.*

- *Take minutes of the meeting and ensure they are distributed timely to those attending,*

- *Make accommodations to support any additional needs of parents. For example, if a parent requires an advocate because of learning diffi- culties, ensure the advocate is invited. Consider whether the parent has any physical difficulties, and they can access the building.*

- *Carry out review meetings within your agency's policies. Understand what the standards and procedures are; for example, there is often a timescale for recording and distributing meeting, or a process for inviting attendees. These are often found on the intranet, or ask you manager about good practice standards.*

Let us turn our attention to the following case study which looks at how you can apply these good practice standards in chairing a review meeting.

CASE STUDY

The following complaint is received by your manager about a meeting you have recently chaired:

Dear Team Manager,

Zoe chaired a review for my daughter Natalie (8 years). I came out of the review 2 hours later feeling very tired and frustrated. I felt that Zoe did not listen to me when I wanted to talk how Natalie was doing at ballet. I have not received any paperwork from the department, and it was not clear what she was talking about in the review meeting. I do not think anything has moved forward for my daughter and this is not acceptable. Dr Walker who is providing play therapy was not there. He is providing a lot of support and without his input the plan/next steps could not be agreed.

Please can these matters be investigated.

Yours sincerely

Natalie's mother.

Reflective question

- *What could be done to improve the meeting?*

Comment

This case study is in the form of a complaint, and with all complaints, it is necessary for the manager or complaints officer to look at the issues raised and determine whether poor practice has happened, and the complaint should be upheld or not. The aim of this case example is to highlight some issues that may come up when arranging and carrying review meetings. For example, should a review meeting take place without the presence of all key stakeholders, (in this example, the play therapist) or are there other ways to include their feedback? Sometimes it is not possible for all professionals to attend a meeting; however, it is important that their feedback be included in some way, i.e. a verbal/written update that can be shared and recorded in the meeting. However, it may be that an important key holder cannot attend a review meeting, and that without their contribution the meeting will be ineffective, and therefore for efficacy, it is appropriate for the meeting to be rearranged. Always discuss and seek guidance from your manager.

Assessing the effectiveness of interventions

Children and families are stakeholders in the child's care plan and hold equal responsibilities to ensure they engage with it and do what is expected of them. However, a parent's level of motivation to engage and quality of their engagement will always be under scrutiny and assessment when considering if the risks to a child are reduced. For positive changes to be embedded, it is important that change is genuine, new behaviours are demonstrated over a sustained period of time and that there is no element of disguised compliance. Disguised compliance is when parents or caregivers give the appearance of cooperation with professionals to allay concerns and end involvement. Therefore, a key part of monitoring intervention plans is assessing whether change has been achieved. We do this by drawing on the principles of assessment and decision-making as discussed in Chapter 4. Consider the following case study, for example.

CASE STUDY

A young mother has had one child (a boy aged 18 months old) removed from her care. This child has been placed for adoption. The care proceedings ended three months before the mother gave birth to another child. The mother is now in care proceedings with her second child, a newborn baby girl. Due to the risks, the baby girl is placed in foster care in the interim. The mother is attending all appointments with the social worker to complete a parenting assessment; she is engaging with a domestic abuse support programme and drug and alcohol services; she obtained a non-molestation order against the child's father. Her engagement with the interventions is seemingly positive. Towards the end of the assessment process, she reports a domestic abuse incident where there is damage to her

---

CASE STUDY *continued*

property. This information is verified from the police. The police report highlights further recent incidents of domestic violence in mother's new relationship and two other incidents where the mother was heavily intoxicated, and police were called for support. The mother has denied being in a relationship during the parenting assessment.

Reflective questions

- *Whilst the mother had done what is expected of her, has her engagement been upfront and truthful?*

- *Has change been achieved?*

- *Have risks to the child reduced?*

Comment

Using our risk and decision-making tool from Chapter 4, from the information you have gathered at the review meetings, you will identify there are still ongoing risks to the child. This case study shows us that in safeguarding practice, we need to assess the impact and outcomes of interventions taking into account information from other professionals.

What happens if we are not achieving outcomes?

Change must be achieved in the child's timescales. This means that children cannot wait indefinitely for parents to make changes. Children need safety and stability to thrive. They need it now, as they are growing and developing, not when their parent or caregiver is ready to provide them with it. When it is assessed that positive change is not being made, the case needs to escalate.

The Children Act 1989 sets out different frameworks for intervention which have a higher level of monitoring as the severity of safeguarding concerns increase. As discussed in Chapter 4, these are:

- Child in Need—when there are concerns around impairment.

- Child Protection—when there are concerns the child is likely to suffer harm.

- Public Law Outline—when there are no changes to the care being given and the local authority is considering going to court

- Care Proceedings—when the child is suffering significant harm. The court has power to provide the highest level of intervention, to remove a child from his or her family or caregivers.

There are formal processes for escalation. For example, for a case to progress from Child in Need to child protection, the Children Act 1989 sets out that a strategy discussion needs to take place and there should be joint decision-making to progress to a Child Protection Conference. The decision for a child to be made subject of a child protection plan is agreed in the first child protection conference. For a case to progress from child protection to Public Law outline, there needs to be a legal planning meeting and for threshold to be crossed. (This is discussed in Chapter 6.)

How will we know if outcomes are achieved?

A good intervention plan will at the start think about the end goal, for example, if there are concerns a child is not being taken to medical appointments, the action might be 'mother to take Jane to all medical appointments. GP to confirm attendance at appointments through email to social worker'. This outcome would be achieved if there is feedback from the GP that all appointments have been attended, and improvements to the child's health observed. However, achieving good outcomes for children is more complicated and when considering whether these have been achieved, further assessment is required. The reasons and importance of this is explained earlier in this chapter.

We must also assess whether it is safe to withdraw support. To do this, we need to once again return to our Safeguarding Assessment and Decision-Making Tool and balance out the risk and protective factors and make judgements on ongoing harm or potential harm to a child. In reaching recommendations on whether ongoing statutory support is required for a child and family, we need to further balance any identified risk factors against the concepts of a child's 'right to family life' and 'good enough parenting'.

Article 8 of the Human Rights Act sets out that your right to private and family life must be respected. Statutory involvement is intrusive and disruptive to family life and there must be clear reasons, such as safeguarding concerns, to become involved with children and families. Intervening with families must be necessary and proportionate.

The concept of "good enough parenting" has been explained earlier in this chapter. Therefore, when balancing risk factors against a child's right to family life, we need to ask the question, Is enough care and support being given to allow a child to be healthy, to be safe, to learn and develop? This is explained further in the following case example.

CASE STUDY

Amelia, aged nine years, has a diagnosis of Downs syndrome, learning difficulties, including speech and language delays, and a heart murmur. She has been subject to a child protection plan due to concerns around her mother's extreme anxiety which means she hasn't been able to leave the house and is fearful something will happen to Amelia if she engages in schooling and other community-based activities. This has resulted in Amelia missing important health appointments and failing to thrive due to lack of educational and social opportunities.

An action of the child protection plan was for mother to engage in psychological support. She was assessed to have attachment anxiety. Mother does not agree with this and has not engaged with any identified intervention. Although not her wish, she has supported Amelia to reintegrate into school and has been taking her to medical appointments.

From home visits, it has been observed that Amelia uses sign language more when communicating, and is benefitting from exposure to a wider environment. Her non-verbal communication is indicating she is happier.

Reflective questions

- *What is the current risk assessment?*

- *Should safeguarding support continue or not? Why?*

Comment

In this case example, although there is still an identified risk, mother's anxiety and this outcome has not been achieved, the impact of this is no longer affecting Amelia. Amelia is going to school where she has social and learning opportunities, and she is communicating her day-to-day experiences. Amelia is linked to universal services which provide a safety net, and should circumstances change, or deteriorate for Amelia, a new referral can be made.

Good assessment skills are a key social work skill and need to be used throughout social work practice to inform decision-making. The tools we provide you with in this book will inform your safeguarding decision-making, and support your professional judgements around thresholds for risk, developing effective interventions, evaluating these interventions and deciding when to escalate safeguarding concerns or to withdraw safeguarding support services.

When it is assessed that good outcomes have been achieved for a child, the reasons for withdrawing support and ending involvement needs to be agreed by the involved professionals, and formally recorded. The mechanisms for recording will differ from local authority to local authority but should usually be recorded in the outcomes form, including where this was jointly decided and a closing case summary.

Diversity and equality in intervention

How you can be mindful of diversity and equality issues in interventions? Consider the following case example.

CASE STUDY

A case is being managed under child protection. Jayden aged 14 years lives alone with his mother. His father has had periods of being in prison and is not involved with him. The family are of Black Caribbean heritage. There are concerns around Jayden's sexualised behaviours, and issues around his poor school attendance and lack of parental supervision and boundary setting. Jayden has a perception that 'all black people end up in prison'. The allocated social worker is from a different culture and the mother makes a request to change the social worker as the mother feels there is a cultural clash.

- *What should happen?*

Comment

Whilst cultural issues should be worked through, in this example, there is merit to a Black Caribbean male being the allocated social worker to Jayden. The social worker would not only be able to provide the identified interventions but also demystify the young boy's beliefs to help motivate his own aspirations.

Interventions and a remote way of working

How does a remote way of working impact on provision of services, and our assessment of the effectiveness of them to the safety and well-being of the children? Consider the following, and discuss with your line manager as necessary.

A drug and alcohol service is offering remote testing. Whilst on a video call with the allocated Drugs and alcohol worker, the parent has to open a sealed envelope, take out a swab, swab their own mouth, place the swab in a new envelope, seal it and return it.	What are the implications of providing a domestic abuse course to a parent, whilst the other parent, the perpetrator, remains in the home?	You are carrying out a statutory visit with a child over a video call.
Will this give an accurate reflection on the parent's alcohol use? Are there gaps?	How might this impact on engagement? How can we be sure the parent is alone/not overheard and not placing themselves at further risk?	How can you ensure the child is on their own?

The COVID-19 pandemic has meant many services providers have had to adapt to a remote way of working too, and aspects of this are likely to be carried forward into future ways of working and service provision. We must not lose sight of our core social work skills. When assessing the impact of interventions, we must also consider the context in which the service/support has been provided and make an analysis of that.

Chapter summary

- Interventions are the support, the change work, offered to make things better and safer for children and young people.

- A social worker needs to formulate intervention plans, monitor their progress and assess the impact of interventions.

- A good intervention plan should set out: what we are worried about, what will be done to address the worry, who will do it, by when and how will we know it has been achieved?

- Children, young people, families and professionals all have responsibilities in achieving the outcomes of the intervention plan.

- We need to use our Safeguarding Assessment and Decision-Making Tool to assess the effectiveness of interventions and when to escalate concerns and when to withdraw support.

YOUR LEARNING JOURNEY

This chapter has focused on interventions and achieving good outcomes for children and young people.

- *From reading this chapter, what have you learned about interventions?*

- *How will you apply this in your practice?*

- *What are the resources/interventions available in your local area? How can you find out about them?*

- *What practice issues could impact on accessing/the availability of interventions? How can you overcome these?*

Chapter 6
Court work

Introduction

Public and Private Law are two legal domains that can be applied to family matters. The focus of this book is on the Local Authority (LA) duties that fall within the domain of public law. Public law in social work has been the subject of enquiry in a recent report *Recommendations to achieve best practice in the child protection & family justice system* (2021), commenting that,

> The steep rise in the issue of public law proceedings seen in 2016/17 and 2017/18 has to some degree eased more recently. But there are still a greater number of cases being issued than in earlier years.
>
> (The Honourable Mr Justice Keehan, 2021: 8–9)

The report was commissioned in response to the increasing number of families involved in child care proceedings and emphasised the negative effects on families, and the professionals involved in the care proceedings system (social workers, solicitors, Cafcass (Children and Family Court Advisory and Support Service) and IRO (Independent Reviewing Officer)). Before exploring the care proceeding process and your role in court, this chapter will define public law and consider what is public law in children and family social work.

Public Law

Public Law is concerned with matters between the state and general public. Public bodies include government bodies and local councils, which use their powers and duties in a variety of areas that can impact the general public. For example, public law in children and family social work refers to how local authorities might use their powers to gather evidence, make decisions and apply for a court order. The purpose of the court order is to ensure that the child/young person's welfare is upheld as paramount and remains the main priority in the family. On a continuum of interventions available to social workers, the application of a court order through care proceedings is at the extreme end of the interventions (see Figure 6.1). The care proceeding process undertaken by the Local Authority can be open to legal challenge if the actions taken are considered to be unlawful or unjust.

The Local Authority involved in care proceedings will endeavour to be transparent and trustworthy when dealing with families. Social workers, supported by their legal representative, gather evidence and present a care proceeding application to request a care order, supervision order or any other court order. This is a complex role, undertaken with dedication, skill and sensitivity. However, there have been a few cases where social workers have been criticised by the Judge about the quality of their case recording and subsequent decision-making concerning a care order application. For example, the case of M & N (Children Local Authority: gathering, preserving and disclosing evidence) [2018] judged, there was 'Wholly inappropriate record keeping in a case that saw a family split for six months'. The care proceeding application had been based on the social worker's recording and decision-making and was brought into question due to the inadequate recording and decision-making. Court work is an intervention that has a lasting impact on all concerned. Therefore, social workers are required to demonstrate their decision-making for seeking a care order, or other court order, in the care proceedings application. As you read through this chapter, we have identified some key areas to help strengthen your decision-making in court work.

Private Law

We will turn now to the Private Law arena in children and families' social work. Private Law is concerned with matters that affect the individual, families or

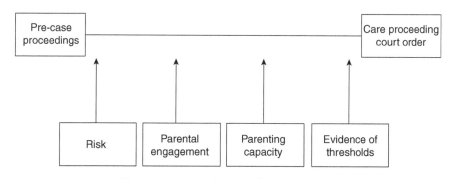

Figure 6.1   Continuum of interventions

businesses. In children and families social work, Private Law may apply if the court is seeking information when determining the correct action to be taken about a child's welfare, such as making decisions on a child's care arrangements, and which parent they should live with and which parent they should spend time with. The court can direct a report under Section 7 of the Children Act 1989, which seeks to assess the welfare issues for the child and makes recommendations about a particular order in proceedings for the care arrangements. The relevant Private Law Orders are explained below:

- *Child Care Arrangements* (whom a child should live with and whom they should spend time with)

- *Prohibited Step Order* (prevents a party of the proceedings from undertaking a certain activity)

- *Specific Issues Order* (An order to address a specific issue that has/may arise about parental responsibility for a child)

- *Family Assistance Order* (A short-term order requesting that the LA or Cafcass officer advise, assist and befriend the person named in the order)

Cafcass is the organisation that undertakes private family law functions and will be directed by the court to complete a Section 7 report under the Children Act 1989 when there are welfare issues for the child or young person that require assessing. A Section 7 report will only be requested from the Local Authority if the child or young person is actively involved with the Local Authority Children's Services department, or the case was closed less than one month before the report is being asked.

In private law proceedings, where there are identified concerns for the welfare of the child, the court can direct the Local Authority to complete a Section 37 report to consider the child's circumstances and whether a care or supervision order is necessary, or whether any services or assistance to the child and family are required.

The private and public law domains recognise that the child's need is at the centre (see Figure 6.2). The relevant professionals involved in the care proceedings, or care arrangements, work together to ensure that the best interests of the child is the primary focus of the proceedings to determine the best course of action or order under the public or private domain.

We will now turn to answer some basic questions and terms about the court process. In the section below, you will be introduced to some of these terms, which you will also come across later in this chapter.

Demystifying Court

Before we consider the roles and responsibilities of the social worker when going to court, and the court process, we will clarify some facts about court for you first.

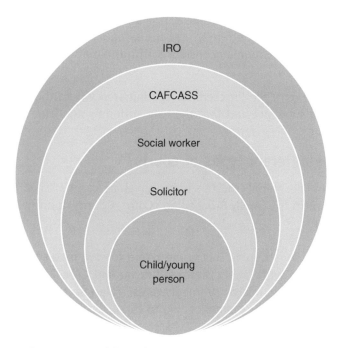

Figure 6.2   Public and Private Law: child at the centre

Why do we go to Court?

We go to court when concerns for the safety and well-being of the child or young person are great, and we need the court to agree an order to protect their welfare. The court application must be based on evidence and the decision-making process.

Under the Children Act 1989, courts have the power to either grant or refuse a Local Authority request for a care order, supervision order or any other order. This responsibility is delegated to magistrates and judges. The Children Act 1989 makes provisions for the 'no order' principle, which emphasises that any decision to apply for a court order should be the very last resort, and that the court should only make an order if it is better for the child than having no order in place, due to the potential for parents to be either permanently excluded from the life of the child or have reduced contact.

What is the difference between Public Law Outline and Care Proceedings?

You need to know the difference between the Public Law Outline and Care Proceedings when undertaking court work. These are explained as follows:

*   *Public Law Outline (PLO)*: This forms part of the family court guidance and sets out how care proceedings should be administered. The Public Law Outline

process is also the pre-court process. It is a formal process in which the Local Authority sets out for the family that the safeguarding concerns are so great that the Local Authority may consider taking the matter to court if no change is achieved.

- *Care Proceedings:* Care Proceedings are initiated where the LA has concerns about a child's welfare and that they are suffering significant harm.

What are the different types of courts?

In England and Wales, family matters or child welfare cases are heard in the Family Court. This can be in the Family Proceedings Court, County Court or Family Division of the High Court:

- *Family Proceedings Court:* This is the name for the magistrates' court when they are dealing with family matters (Brayne and Carr, 2008: 30). The court application will be heard by magistrates, referred to as 'Your Worship'. Magistrates are usually a panel of two to three specially trained persons, who are advised by a legal clerk.

- *County Court:* Cases are heard by Circuit Judges, Recorders, District Judges, Deputy District Judges. Judges are referred to as 'Your Honour'. Cases are transferred up from the magistrates' Court to County Court (or High Court), based on the complexity of the case. The court will decide this upon receiving and allocating the case.

- *Family Division of High Court:* The High Court has the power to hear all cases relating to children. In practice, it hears the more complex cases under the Children Act 1989. The High Court hears appeals against decisions of magistrates' and the county courts (Brayne and Carr, 2008: 30)

Who are the people who go to Court and what are their roles?

The people who go to court are:

- Social workers/team managers, on behalf of the Local Authority, to raise the safeguarding concerns to the court.

- Parents, or any one with parental responsibility. They will put across their position in relation to the issues raised.

- Children's guardian, on behalf of Cafcass, to represent the child's wishes and feelings and make independent recommendations on what is in the child's best interests.

- Solicitors/barristers, who respectively represent each, the Local Authority, parents and child, through their appointed Children's Guardian. Solicitors are different to barristers. Solicitors do the legal work outside of court, and barristers do the speaking at court.

These are the adults who go to court. What about children and young people? Let us consider this in the following activity.

- *Do children and young people go to court?*

Comment

Court cases evoke complex and powerful emotions and therefore whether a child attends court is dependent on the child's age, level of understanding of the safeguarding concerns and competency. Children and young people are central to the court process, and it is important that what they want to happen is heard by the court. Provisions for this are made by the appointment of a Children's Guardian. Children and young people can attend court and speak directly to the judge or write a letter to the judge to get their views heard. With older children, sometimes what they want to happen is different to what their Children's Guardian assesses to be in their best interests. In such circumstances, if they are assessed as competent to give instructions, which is an assessment/judgement made by the child's solicitor, the solicitor remains for the child and not the children's guardian, to ensure the child's views are heard.

What are some common terms used in court work?

Here are some words you may come across in court work:

- *Application:* Submitting a report to the court to request that they grant an order

- *Applicant:* The person making the court application, usually Children Services Department of the Local Authority.

- *Respondents:* Those who are named on the application and have parental responsibility. Respondents are entitled to copy of the application.

- *Party to Proceedings:* Any person who is affected by the care proceedings. This includes children and young people who are party to proceedings through their Children's Guardian. In some cases, anyone may raise objections to the application and request to be part of the proceedings.

How do we prepare for Court?

Going to court is a legal process, and as a social worker, you will be instructing a solicitor, usually employed within the Local Authority you work for, to be the lead in this process. There will be tasks that the solicitor will need to do, and tasks that you as a social worker need to do. These tasks will be explained in more detail throughout this chapter. Before making an application to the court, you will need to establish whether you have grounds to go to court. Let's look at what we mean by this in the following reflective question.

REFLECTIVE QUESTION

In court work, you will hear the terms Threshold *and* Welfare.

- *What do these terms mean and why are they important in court work?*

Threshold

When preparing for court, the primary consideration is whether threshold is crossed. Threshold is defined in Section 31 of the Children Act 1989 as follows:

a. that the child concerned is suffering, or is likely to suffer, significant harm and

b. that the harm, or likelihood of harm, is attributable to the following:

> i. the care given to the child, or likely to be given to him if the order were not made, not being what it would be reasonable to expect a parent to give to him; or

> ii. the child's being beyond parental control.

You need to understand this definition of threshold as it will be relevant in court work in the following ways:

Before an application is made, you will need to seek legal advice around whether threshold is met. This usually happens in a Legal Planning Meeting. The Legal Planning Meeting includes the Local Authority solicitor, the allocated social worker and senior manager to decide if there is sufficient evidence of harm to meet threshold criteria. If the threshold criteria are met, the LA will make an application to the court, and decide what steps they will be taking, i.e. to initiate the Public Law Outline process, or Care Proceedings.

If a decision is made at the Legal Planning Meeting, that the Local Authority should issue care proceedings, your solicitor will make an application to the court, which must be supported by:

- *Social work reports*, including a genogram, chronology, statement and care plan. These are explained later in the chapter. In summary, the supporting social work documents must set out the background to the case, the social work analysis of the risks a child is exposed to, what orders you are asking the court to make and what the proposed care arrangements for the child will be.

- *Threshold document.* A Threshold Document is a legal document prepared by the Local Authority legal representation, which sets out the facts the Local Authority will seek to prove by evidence or concession that the child has suffered or is likely to suffer significant harm (Family Procedure Rule, Practice Direct 12A).

The court needs to determine that threshold is crossed to become involved in decision-making for child and young people, and to make a Care or Supervision Order. A judge will refer to this when giving a judgement.

The parents/carers need to respond to the Threshold Document, setting out whether they accept or do not accept the identified risks of significant harm. If threshold is not accepted, it means the court will need to make findings on the harm the child has experienced. The standard of proof used in court is the balance of probabilities. This means, based on the evidence before the court, it is more likely than not the child will suffer harm.

Welfare

You already know from our earlier chapters that the child's welfare is of paramount importance. When the court makes decisions, it needs to not only consider whether threshold is crossed, but whether the child's welfare requires the court to make decisions for them. As a social worker, you will need to address the welfare issues for the child in your reports to court. These are set out in Section 1 of the Children Act 1989 as follows:

a. the ascertainable wishes and feelings of the child concerned (considered in the light of his age and understanding);

b. his physical, emotional and educational needs;

c. the likely effect on him of any change in his circumstances;

d. his age, sex, background and any characteristics of his which the court considers relevant;

e. any harm which he has suffered or is at risk of suffering;

f. how capable each of his parents, and any other person in relation to whom the court considers the question to be relevant, is of meeting his needs;

g. the range of powers available to the court under this Act in the proceedings in question.

For the court to make an order, the court needs to consider that doing so would be better for the child than making no order at all (Children Act 1989). Therefore, a thorough assessment of the welfare issues will set out for the court why the making of an order is in the child's bests interests. When making any orders, the court must consider the Human Rights Act 1998 and ensure their intervention is necessary and proportionate to the risks identified to the child. But what do we mean by these terms?

- *Necessary:* the court must be convinced that the child's immediate safety requires an order to be made.

- *Proportionate:* the court must be satisfied that all other options have been considered, and that what the court is being asked to do, for example, make an Interim Care Order for separation, is the only option.

These principles can be understood by considering this case situation. The Local Authority makes an application for an Interim Care Order for a newborn baby due to concerns around the mother's long-standing and complex mental health needs. The care plan is separation, and for the baby to be placed in foster care. The court may identify that threshold is met, and that the risks identified are such that it is necessary for an order to be made, the child's immediate safety requires it. However, if the Local Authority has not demonstrated that separation is the only option and explained the reasons why, for example, a mother baby placement or alternative family placement, is not appropriate, the care plan of separation may not be assessed by the court as proportionate. The court could either adjourn the hearing for the Local Authority to provide further information to meet the pro-portionality element of making an order; or endorse a different care plan.

We have been talking about the Welfare checklist. What about cases where adoption is being put forward as the care plan? Let's consider this in the following activity.

ACTIVITY 6.1

Look up the Adoption checklist in the Adoption and Children Act 2002 at: https:// www.legislation.gov.uk/ukpga/2002/38/section/1.

- *How is the Adoption checklist different or the same to the Welfare Checklist?*

Comment

Doing this activity, you will see that there is a separate Adoption Checklist. Adoption puts forward the severance of the child's relationships with their birth family. The Adoption Checklist makes provisions for an analysis of these factors. Before making an Adoption Order, the court must consider whether there should be arrangements for allowing any person contact with the child (The Children and Family Act, 2004). Therefore there needs to be an assessment of the important relationships to the child, and whether these should be continued.

What are the reports a social worker needs to prepare for Court?

When making an application to the court, the PLO sets out in the pre-proceedings checklist that the social worker needs to provide their solicitor with the following documents to be filed with the court/parties:

- *Chronology:* this is a succinct summary of the length of involvement the Local Authority has had with the child and family; and the significant events of the child's life, set out in chronological order.

- *Genogram:* this is a visual depiction of the family relationships.

- *Statement:* this is an assessment/report of the risks the child is exposed to.

- *Care Plan:* this identifies the proposed care arrangements for the child (i.e. where they will live), and how child's care needs will be met.

The principles of assessment and report writing, such as good analysis, distinguishing between fact and professional opinion or assessment, and evidenced-based and defensible decision-making (as discussed in Chapter 3) apply when writing court reports. Please refer to them when writing your court reports.

We will now use the following activity to look at what should be included in your social work statement and care plan.

ACTIVITY **6.2**

Social work statement

The Local Authority you work for will have a template for you to use when writing your social work genogram, chronology, statement and care plan. This can be accessed from your legal representative, or team manager.

ADCS (The Association of Directors of Children's Services) and Cafcass (Children and Family Court Advisory and Support Service) developed the Social Work Evidence Template (SWET, 2014), which has been updated in 2016 and 2021. The SWET was designed to support a consistent, analytical approach to presenting social work evidence to the family courts and sets out key areas a social work statement should cover. Whilst more and more local authorities are using this, it is not mandatory. However, it is good template to consider when developing your skills in preparing and writing social work statements.

Look up the SWET at https://adcs.org.uk/care/article/SWET.

- *What do you think are the key elements a social work statement should set out?*

Comment

Your social work statement needs to clearly set out the order/s sought; the family composition; the background to the case; the current risks/harm to the child including an assessment of parenting capacity and child impact analysis, with reference to the welfare checklist; what support you have provided to address the risks and why the application is being made now; what assessment you are seeking within the proceedings, and what the proposed care arrangements are for the child; including contact proposals.

ACTIVITY 6.3

Care plan

The Children Act 1989 guidance and regulations Volume 2: Care planning, placement and case review gives guidance on what the contents of a care plan should be.

Look this up at https://assets.publishing.service.gov.uk/government/uploads/system/uploads/attachment_data/file/441643/Children_Act_Guidance_2015.pdf.

- *Note down what you think should be included in the care plan.*

Comments

Care plans are usually set out in five sections as follows:

- Overall aim and timetable;
- Child's needs, including contact, health, social and cultural needs;
- View of others, especially parents—and reasons for discounting those view if not followed;
- Placement details and timetable and
- Management and support to be provided by the Local Authority.

Of utmost importance, you need to have a clear plan for the child, either in the interim (i.e. during the proceedings) or in the long term (i.e. the plan for permanence for the child at the end of proceedings). The court cannot make an order until it can assess what the proposed care plan for the child is. The care arrangements for the child are protected through the making of a court order.

What are the range of orders you can ask the court to make?

When making an application to the court, you need to be clear about what order you are asking the court to make. The range of Public Law Orders are set out in Section 31 of The Children Act 1989. The range of Private Law Orders are set out in Section 8 of The Children Act 1989. Table 6.1 provides you with a list of orders you are most likely to come across in your safeguarding role.

Table 6.1   Common court orders in Public Law Proceedings

No Order	Section 31 of the Children Act 1989 identifies that court should only make an order if doing so is better for the child than making no order at all. There may be times when the court assesses that No Order is better for the child.
Supervision Order/Interim Supervision Order	A Supervision Order puts the child or young person under the supervision of the Local Authority (LA). A Supervision Order gives the LA powers to advise, assist and befriend the supervised child. Parental responsibility remains with the parent/carer. (Section 31 of the Children Act 1989)
Care Order/Interim Care Order	A Care Order places the child in the care of a designated LA. The LA shares parental responsibility with the parents. An Interim Care Order can be made when the child's immediate safety requires it. (Section 31 of the Children Act 1989)
Emergency Protection Order	This order is only made when there are reasonable grounds to consider the child is likely to suffer significant harm. It gives powers to the applicant (either LA or other) to accommodate the child in a safe place, or prevents the child from being taken from their safe accommodation, i.e. a hospital. It gives the applicant parental responsibility for the child. Emergency Protection Orders last eight days (Section 44 of the Children Act 1989)
Special Guardianship Order	A Special Guardianship Order appoints one or more individuals to be a child's 'special guardian' (or special guardians). The Special Guardian is awarded parental responsibility through the making of the order (Section 14 of the Children Act 1989)
Child Arrangements Order	A Child Arrangement is an order which sets out who the child lives with, spends time with or otherwise has contact with (Section 8 of the children Act 1989)
Placement Order/Care order	A Placement Order is an order made by the court authorising an LA to place a child for Adoption with any prospective adopters who may be chosen by the authority. A placement order can only be made if the LA has a Care Order. A placement order continues until an Adoption Order is made (Section 31 of the Children Act 1989)

(Continued)

Table 6.1 (Continued)

Adoption Order	An Adoption Order gives parental responsibility for a child to the adopters or adopter. Before making an Adoption Order, the court must consider whether there should be arrangements for allowing any person contact with the child (Adoption and Children Act 2002)

Now that you know some of the different orders a court can make, let us see how we can apply these in practice. Remember, your recommendations to the court, and the making of any order, needs to be necessary and proportionate to the assessed risk.

ACTIVITY 6.4

Think about the definitions and principles of each of the above orders and consider the following case examples. Write down which order you think is necessary and proportionate to the case example.

Case example	Order
Case example 1 Suzy is nine years old. She has experienced instability in her caregiving. Mary (Suzy's mother) experienced post-natal depression and struggled to bond with Suzy. She was seventeen years old when she had Suzy and found it difficult to prioritise Suzy's needs above her own. She had unrealistic expectations of caring for a new-born baby. The maternal grandmother was granted a Child Arrangements Order for Suzy to live with her when Suzy was two years old. Suzy lived with her maternal grandmother from 2 to 6 years old. Suzy experienced harm in the maternal grandmother's care, including concerns around the maternal grandmother's drugs use, and neglect of Suzy. Suzy was displaying difficult behaviours and emotions at school. Suzy was returned to her mother's care. At this time, Mary had started a relationship with Zack. Mary and Zack had Joshua, a boy. They looked after Joshua together, with Suzy, but the LA was involved due to concerns around domestic abuse within the relationship between Mary and Zack, and parental cannabis use. Attachment work was provided between Mary and Suzy. Care proceedings have been issued due to concerns that domestic violence incidents have escalated, and despite support, no change is being made. There are concerns around Suzy's emotional and behavioural presentation. Mary fled domestic violence to a refuge. Suzy went to stay with her paternal grandfather, whom she has a good relationship so she could continue going to school and not be disrupted. Joshua remained in Mary's care during care proceedings under an Interim Supervision Order. Joshua had supervised contact with his father, Zack. This has been positive.	

Case example	Order
During proceedings, Suzy has been living with her paternal grandfather and his partner under fostering regulations. Suzy has always had a good relationship with him. Suzy has continued to see her mum at contact and has expressed that 'mum does not understand her'. Suzy is conflicted in not wanting to upset her mother by saying she has better experiences with paternal grandfather. A positive special guardianship assessment has been completed on the paternal grandfather and his partner. Mary wants Suzy to return to her care and has made some changes during proceedings. Mary has separated from Zack reducing exposure of domestic abuse, and hair strand testing suggests Mary has stopped using all substances. Joshua has remained in her care, and he is meeting developmental milestones. Zack has continued to address his substances misuse. There remains animosity between Mary and Zack and disputes around how contact between Zack and Joshua should progress. **What are the necessary and proportionate orders to recommend for each Suzy and Joshua in this case scenario?**	
Case example 2 The LA receives a referral from Accident and Emergency. A girl aged two years has attended with significant head injuries. There have been inconsistent accounts as to how she sustained them. There is high suspicion the injuries are non-accidental. The girl requires further medical assessment and intervention. The parents want to discharge her against medical advice. **What should the Local Authority do?**	
Case example 3 The children are two boys: Ryan aged ten years and Paul aged nine years. Ryan has a communication disorder and has difficulties making himself understood; he displays challenging behaviours. Ryan attends a school for children with social, emotional and behaviour needs. There are concerns that Ryan is sustaining recurring injuries, and that the parents cannot manage the children's behaviours. Three child protection medicals have been undertaken on Ryan which raise concerns around parenting capacity and that the behaviours are environmental. At school, and in the community when with his carers, Ryan's behaviours are managed with consistent routines and boundaries. Ryan enters care under a voluntary Section 20 agreement of the Children Act 1989. Paul attends a mainstream school but is behind age-related expectation. Two weeks after Ryan went into care, Paul sustains a further non-accidental injury whilst he is in his parents' care. There are inconsistencies in how he sustained this injury. Paul now has a second child protection medical. Parents agree for Paul to go into care under a voluntary Section 20 Agreement of the Children Act 1989. Parents continue to work with the LA, but decisions need to be made on the long-term care plans for Ryan and Paul. **The children are already in care; is an Interim Care Order necessary and proportionate?**	

(Continued)

Case example	Order
Case example 4 The LA has the following immediate concerns for the three children aged 7 years, 5 years and 3 years: • Mother has a history of being in relationships where there is domestic abuse. • Mother is in new relationship, where there are concerns that her partner is a risky individual. He is known to the police for having offensive weapons and allegations of sexual abuse. He has unmanaged mental health needs with a history of paranoid conspiracies. Mother has chosen to remain in the relationship despite being made aware of the risks her partner presents to the children's welfare. • Mother has changed from engaging with the social worker to refusing access. • Mother read a statement to the social worker stating 'she was queen of the land'. It is believed she was being forced to do this by her partner. • Police completed a visit to the partner's property and found the mother and children staying in one bedroom; child pornography, air rifles and knuckle dusters were found at the property too. • Mother maintained the children were safe and her partner did not present any risk. • The police placed the children under Police Powers of Protection. This lasts for 48 hours. **The matter is listed for an urgent case management hearing. What order should the LA be applying for?**	
Case example 5 The children are Alex, an eighteen-month-old boy, and Josephine, a three-year-old girl. Care proceedings were initiated due to concerns around: • Domestic abuse in the parental relationship. There are a high number of police call-outs. Josephine experienced her mother being assaulted by her father. • A large amount of professional support has been provided through Child In Need, Child Protection and PLO processes, with no change being achieved. • Neglect: Josephine regularly sustains minor injuries due to a lack of parental supervision. • Parenting: mother struggles to manage challenging behaviours and put in boundaries. During the proceedings: • The paternal grandparents are assessed as a positive support and Alex and Josephine stay two nights per week with them. Mother admits she benefits from this. A positive special guardianship assessment has been completed on them. • Mother has completed a domestic abuse intervention programme and is demonstrating insight into this. • There is a reduction in A&E attendances. • The Health Visitor has no concerns around the child's health and development. Mother is taking on board parenting advice.	

Case example	Order
• Father is sofa surfing and sees the children when they are spending time with the paternal grandparents. • Father is not putting himself forward as a caregiver due to his lack of accommodation. • A positive parenting assessment has been completed on the father. **What is an appropriate care plan for the children?**	
Case example 6 The LA makes an application for an Interim Care Order for a new-born baby. The identified risks are: • Mother has experienced childhood trauma, including experiencing neglectful parenting. Her parenting is untested. • Mother has a diagnosis of Borderline Personality Disorder. Her mental health is stable, and she engages well with mental health services. • Mother used cannabis daily before finding out she was pregnant. She has stopped all drug and alcohol use since being pregnant. • Father smokes cannabis daily. • Mother and father live with paternal grandfather and paternal great grandmother. There are concerns around the volatility of the home environment. The paternal great grandmother has a diagnosis of Alzheimer's and there are regular police call-outs and allegations and cross allegations of assaults. This would be frightening for a new-born baby. The paternal great grandfather is currently in hospital following a fall. • The support network is not tested out. • Both parents are engaging with family support worker **What is the most proportionate and necessary order?**	
Case example 7 The children are a boy aged fourteen years, and a girl aged twelve years. They are half-siblings and have been adopted. This was their care plan following public law proceedings when they were babies; their birth mother was unable to give them consistent and safe care. The LA became involved when the children made disclosures through Child Line of physical and emotional abuse, and neglect of their health needs by their adopted parents. The children have maintained that this is their experience during proceedings. Their adopted parents dispute this and have not engaged in reparative work or put themselves forward for further assessment to support reunification. Assessment within proceedings identify the impact of their parenting on their sibling relationship and individual needs of each child. **What is an appropriate final order for the children?**	

Comment

Here are the answers. Discuss these with your line manager if necessary.

Case example 1: Special Guardianship Order for Suzy; Child Arrangements Order for Joshua; Supervision Order for both children

Case example 2: Emergency Protection Order

Case example 3: No order, continue with Section 20 Agreement of the Children Act 1989

Case example 4: Interim Care Order

Case example 5: Child Arrangements Order

Case example 6: Supervision Order

Case example 7: Care Order

We hope you found this exercise useful. When making recommendations about the most appropriate order, you need to balance out the factors for and against each order, taking into the account the individual needs of each child, and the family and environment factors. For example, a child might be placed in a family placement. This could be secured through either the making of a Care Order, or the making of a Special Guardianship Order. Factors such as the intrusion of ongoing statutory involvement through a Care Order as the child will remain subject to child looked after procedures must be balanced against the child's right to family life. Or it may be that the family dynamics are complex, and a Care Order better promotes placement stability and protects the family placement from risks of breakdown when family relationship cannot be managed under a Special Guardianship Order.

When putting forth care plans and recommendations for sibling groups, it is equally important not to lose sight of the needs of the individual children, and whether they should be placed together or apart as in case example 1. In another example, consider the care plans for a sibling group consisting of an eighteen-month-old, four-year-old and eight-year-old. You may assess the children have good sibling bonds and awareness of each other. However, adoption is usually not considered appropriate for children over the age of five years. The younger siblings need for permanence and to settle into a forever family through Adoption will need to be balanced against the benefits of an ongoing sibling relationship through a care plan of long-term foster care, which is liable to be intrusive from going statutory and high risk of multiple placements moves.

What happens at Court?

To consider what happens at court, we must remind ourselves about the purposes of going to court. Ultimately, we go to court to achieve permanence for the child. By this we mean our goal is for a child or young person to know where they will be living in the long term, and to ensure that the identified placement will meet their welfare needs and allow them to thrive and reach their potential. The Children Act 1989 guidance and regulation Volume 2: care planning, placement and case review (2015; page 22) defines permanence as 'ensuring that children have a secure, stable and loving family to support them through childhood and beyond and to give them a sense of security, continuity, commitment, identity and belonging'.

The court acknowledges the impact of proceedings and the anxiety and disruption of not knowing on children and families. Under the PLO guidance, the court has responsibility to conclude cases within twenty-six weeks.

Your solicitor will guide you through the court process by following the Family Procedure Rules. The family procedure rules are a single set of rules governing the practice and procedure in family proceedings in the high court, county courts and magistrates' courts.

We will now turn out attention to what happens at court to enable the court to make the final decision about the long-term care arrangements for the child.

What are the different types of hearings?

Practice Direction 12A of the Family Procedures Rules gives guidance on the court process. There are four stages:

- Stage 1: Issues and Allocations
- Stage 2: Case Management
- Stage 3: Issues Resolution
- Stage 4: Final Hearing

The process of proceeding can be likened to an 'assessment phase' and a time for solicitors to become trial ready. The different type of hearings in the court process each has a clear purpose to progress the case. To help you understand what happens at court, we will explain the different court hearings, using a case example to bring this to life for you.

CASE STUDY: MARCUS

The Local Authority makes an application for an Interim Care Order for Marcus, a newborn baby. The Social Work Chronology and Statement sets out that he is at risk of suffering significant harm due to:

- *The mother's mental health: she has a history of suicide ideation, and during pregnancy, she was self-harming with scissors and jumped from a moving van.*

- *The mother has a history of seeking out relationships with risky and unsafe adults. Her last three relationships have been domestically abusive where she has experienced significant physical abuse, regular police calls-outs and was confined to the property, save for going shopping.*

- *The mother has suspected learning difficulties and has not understood the need for preparation pre-birth. She has had periods where she has neglected herself.*

(Continued)

> ### CASE STUDY: MARCUS continued
>
> - *The putative father is homeless and is a known drug user. He flags in police records for violence and domestic abuse.*
>
> - *Mother is known to children's services as a child and was a child looked after due to concerns of parental alcohol use and domestic violence.*
>
> - *Father is known to children's services as a child and was placed on a child protection plan for physical injury and parental cannabis use.*
>
> - *Mother has put forward a friend to support her looking after Marcus. The Local Authority has completed a Viability Assessment, which is negative. Mother has known the friend for five months. The friend has an addiction to prescription drugs and is open to a drug support service. She is sofa surfing and has not demonstrated insight into the concerns mother presents.*

Let us follow this case example through the court process.

Stage 1: Issues and allocation

This is the first stage when the relevant documents are filed with the court, and the court issues an application.

In the case example, the social work chronology, genogram, statement and care plan have been filed through the Local Authority solicitor setting out the concerns as per case example.

Stage 2: First hearing/case management hearing

A case is first heard at a Case Management Hearing. This takes place not before day 12 and not later than day 18 (Practice Direction 12A, FPR). A request for an urgent hearing can be made when the circumstances of the case require direction on an immediate issue. For example, in the matter of Marcus, mother wants to parent Marcus at home, but the Local Authority is worried about this. The court needs to decide on where Marcus should be placed upon discharge from hospital. This decision cannot wait. A hearing to deal specifically with this issue is held at the first available opportunity.

> ### CASE STUDY: MARCUS
>
> *The court lists the application for an urgent hearing, and upon hearing the evidence from all parties, supports the Local Authority's care plan for in Interim Care Order and for Marcus to be placed with his mother in a mother and baby foster placement.*

> CASE STUDY: MARCUS *continued*
>
> *In Case Management hearings, the court will determine the interim arrangements for the child, i.e. where the child should live during the process of proceedings. At a Case Management hearing, the court must draw up the timetable for the child and the timetable for the proceedings. This means the court must consider what information it needs to be able to make a final decision for the child. It will give directions on the assessments and work to be undertaken during proceedings and set dates for when the work must be completed by. You should leave the hearing with a clear timetable of when expert assessments will be filed, when you must file evidence, when parents must file evidence and when the next court hearings will be.*
>
> ### Reflective question
>
> • *What are the different assessments a court can direct to ensure it is fully informed at the final hearing?*

Comment

To answer this, we need to go back to the identified risk factors and think about what evidence or assessments can provide an understanding of the impact of the risk on the child.

Some common assessments/evidence filed in proceedings might include the following:

- DNA testing, to determine paternity;

- Hair strand testing, to assess the level of drug and alcohol use;

- Psychological/psychiatric assessments to understand personality functioning/mental health and identify any clinical disorders, and treatment prognosis;

- Parenting assessment, to assess parenting capacity. This can be completed either by the allocated Social Worker or Independent Social Worker (ISW);

- Child psychiatric assessment, to assess the children mental health needs;

- Paediatric assessments, to determine any health needs;

- Cognitive assessment, to determine level of learning needs;

- Domestic violence risk assessments, to determine the level of risk a person presents to parent or child;

- Viability assessments on any person put forward, to consider whether a full assessment is required;

- Special guardianship assessment, to consider the long-term suitability of family/friends to provide care;

- Fostering assessment;
- Sibling assessment, to assess the individual needs of the child and whether sibling should be placed together or apart;
- Directions for police disclosures;
- Directions for disclosure of medical records.

Due process must be followed for a court to direct an assessment/disclosure of information. This is explained in the following reflective question.

REFLECTIVE QUESTION

- *What is a Part 25 Application?*

Comment

This is a term you are likely to hear in court. Any party can make an application for an expert assessment, but this must be applied through a Part 25 application. This is the responsibility of your legal representative. As a social worker, you will give instruction on what assessments you want to be undertaken to progress your case, and your preference on which professionals/expert should complete the assessment. The court will have the final say on directing the assessment and determining the professional to undertake it.

Let's turn back to the case study of Marcus.

CASE STUDY: MARCUS

Further information:

Paternity testing of the father was directed at the urgent hearing. The putative father has been confirmed as the biological father. He is not putting himself forward to care for Marcus but wants to be involved in his life through contact.

ACTIVITY 6.5

- *Considering the risks identified in the case, what Part 25 applications would you request your solicitor to make? Write these down.*

Comment

Considering the issues in the case, the following assessments are proportionate and necessary.

- Viability assessments on the family and friends put forward. If any of these are positive, special guardianship assessment is to be progressed;

- Cognitive and psychological assessment on mother;

- Hair strand testing on father;

- Risk assessment of father;

- Parenting assessment of mother.

Any party can make an application for a Further Case Management Hearing (FCMH) during proceedings if there are issues that need resolving. However, an FCMH should only be directed where necessary and must not be regarded as a routine step in proceedings.

Let us return to our case study of Marcus to consider one circumstance where a FCMH might be necessary.

CASE STUDY: MARCUS

Further Information:

A viability assessment is completed on the paternal grandmother (Iris) and paternal aunt (Amber). They live together and are putting themselves forward to jointly care for Marcus. The viability assessment raises concerns that:

- *The father has made threats to petrol-bomb their property. They have not acted protectively, i.e. followed through with Non-molestations Orders. There are questions whether they will be able to protect Marcus from further threats/harm.*

- *The father and Amber have been subject to child protection plans. What changes are there to Iris' parenting capacity?*

- *Amber has experienced sexual abuse and was not protected from this by Iris.*

- *Iris experienced termination of contract due to allegation of excessive force.*

Reflective question

- *Iris and Amber wish to challenge the outcome of the assessment. How can they do this?*

Comment

In this circumstance there is a dispute. The Local Authority is saying there should not be a further assessment of Iris and Amber, but the father is saying there should be. The parties need direction from the court as to the way forward. It is appropriate for the father, through his solicitor, to make an application for a Case Management Hearing and lodge a Part 25 Application for a Special Guardianship Assessment of the paternal grandmother (Iris) and paternal aunt (Amber).

In this case, the court did not find merit in progressing a special guardianship assessment due to the identified risk factors. The court dismissed the application.

Stage 3: Issues resolution hearing

The issues resolution hearing (IRH) takes place before the Final Hearing and the purpose is to consider what are the issues agreed and what are the matters the Court needs to decide. It also discusses how the Final Hearing will proceed, for example, who will be required to give evidence, and what the time allocations are for this.

In some cases, care arrangements may be agreed for the child at the IRH, and the court will endorse these. In other cases, they are not, and the case must progress to a contested final hearing, where the court will hear evidence from all parties.

Let's see what happens at this stage of proceedings in our case study of Marcus.

CASE STUDY: MARCUS

Further information:

The evidence gathered in proceedings is as follows:

- *Cognitive assessment identifies mother has learning needs.*

- *Psychological assessment identifies mother remains vulnerable to depression and emotional instability. There are real risks of her engaging in risky behaviour including self-harm, or having a lack of motivation to do any daily living tasks.*

- *Parenting assessment is negative. The mother has not been able to meet the care needs of Marcus without a high level of support from the foster carer. She can do something if part of the routine, but not through being intuitive or attentive or responsive to the baby's needs.*

- *Risk assessment of father is a medium risk to Marcus and contact should continue as supervised.*

- *Hair Strand Testing of father is positive for cocaine and cannabis, and chronic excessive alcohol use.*

- *The mother has remained vulnerable to relationships that are domestically abusive. Notwithstanding her history of domestic abuse relationships, she started a relationship during proceedings which she was dishonest about, where she gave her money to her partner, meaning she did not have money to buy Marcus nappies and formula. Her new partner is a known drug user.*

- *Five viability assessments have been completed. They are all negative.*

ACTIVITY 6.6

Returning to Activity 6.5 on recommending necessary and proportionate orders, considering the facts of this case, what orders do you think the Local Authority should be pursuing?

Comment

Considering the above evidence, Care and Placement Orders are appropriate. The test of nothing else will do has been met and all options to keep Marcus in the family placement have been explored and assessed as not viable.

Let's see what happens next in our case example.

CASE STUDY: MARCUS

Further information:

The parties' positions at the IRH are as follows:

Local Authority: Are putting forward a care plan of adoption and are seeking Care Orders and Placement Order for Marcus. Mother continues to present a high risk and there are no family or friends who can support her in her caring role.

Mother: Makes an application to live with her sister who can support her in her parenting role. A negative viability assessment has been completed, which the sister wishes to challenge.

Father: Is not putting himself forward. He remains neutral on care plans.

Guardian: Supports Local Authority care plans.

Comment

There are contested matters, and the case progresses to a Final Hearing.

Stage 4: Final hearing

The Final Hearing is the final stage of proceedings. At the Final Hearing, the court will consider all the evidence and make final decisions for the child or young person. At the final hearing, the written evidence, often referred to in legal terms as 'evidence in chief', will be tested out through examination and cross-examination of the witnesses. The court will usually hear oral evidence when there are facts that are disputed and need to be proved. The purpose of oral evidence is for the court to hear each witness's account and decide which they prefer or believe is the truth. This will be balanced against the written evidence before the court.

The final decision is delivered in a judgement where the judge will address the threshold issues and welfare issues for the child and give the court's reasons for the decisions it makes.

Giving oral evidence

When it is necessary for a court to hear oral evidence to make a final decision, the order is usually as follows:

- The applicant: Local Authority social worker;
- Any experts, such a psychologists, paediatrician, etc.;
- The respondents, for example, the mother, father and any other relevant carer;
- Children's guardian.

Before giving evidence, you will be asked to say the Oath. This is to swear or affirm to the court that what you tell the court will be the truth.

The three stages of giving oral evidence are as follows:

- *Examination:* Your solicitor will ask you to confirm your name, professional role and address, and ask you to confirm that you are the author of the written evidence and that the facts are true. You are unlikely to be asked further questions, unless it is to update the court on new matters that have arisen since your written evidence was filed.

- *Cross-examination:* This is when you are asked questions on your evidence in chief (your written evidence) on behalf of the other parties. It is when the testing out of your evidence takes place.

- *Re-examination:* When your solicitor will come back to you with further questions, if anything is raised in cross-examination.

PRACTICE TIPS FOR GIVING EVIDENCE

Speaking in court can be nerve-racking, and therefore, here are some tips to give you confidence when giving oral evidence.

- *Know your case and be confident in your position and reasons for it.*

- *You are being asked questions on your written evidence, and therefore do not go beyond this, or fact, or expertise.*

- *Be familiar with and read all relevant documents in the court bundle.*

- *Address the judge/magistrates when answering questions. Refer to a Circuit Judge as 'Your Honour', District Judge as 'Sir/Madam', Magistrates as 'Your Worships'.*

- *Speak slowly and clearly.*

- *Be ready for cross-examination techniques:*
  - *You may be asked multifaceted questions; it's okay to ask the advocate to break these down.*
  - *You may be asked questions which are incomprehensible; it's okay to say 'I don't understand'.*
  - *You may be asked questions which are hypothetical; it's okay to say 'I can't answer that' or 'I don't know'.*

- *Remain calm and do not become emotional or lose your temper.*

- *It's okay to pause and think before giving a response.*

- *Be measured; don't be afraid to say the positives.*

Contact

A key consideration in court work is contact. Contact is the time the child spends with their parents/carer. The Children Act 1989 sets out duties for the Local Authority to provide the child reasonable contact with their parents/carers and those important to the child. Therefore, careful consideration must be given to the level of relationship the child has with their parent/carer during proceedings (if interim separation is agreed), or once final orders are made. When you unpack the issues of contact, you will see that just like assessing risk is complex, assessing contact is complex, too. We need to look at the individual factors for each child and family when making recommendations for contact. We will now turn our attention to how to make safe contact recommendations.

Risks and benefits to contact

To help develop your thinking about the complexity of contact, let us first spend some time thinking about the benefits and risk to contact.

What do you think are the benefits and risks to contact? Write these down.

Comment

Through our own experience, and drawing on the finding from the paper *Managing Risks and Benefits of Contact* (DofE, Research in Practice, 2014), we have identified some benefits and risks to contact as follows:

Benefits to contact:

- Contact maintains an existing relationship, which is important to the child's or young person's sense of identity.

- Contact lessens feelings of rejection for the child or young person if they are still able to see their parent or carer. It shows them they are not forgotten.

- Contact lessens anxiety for the child or young person by giving the child some reassurances that their parent/carer is well.

- Contact keeps the child informed of any changes in their birth family.

Risks to contact:

- There is the potential to expose the child to further harm both directly or indirectly

- There is the potential to re-enact unresolved attachments, which can be disruptive on the child's ability to recover from harm.

- Contact can diminish the progress a child makes in placement.

- If the frequency of contact is too high, it can be disruptive and impact on the child's ability to experience consistent care giving in placement and settle into placement.

What factors impact contact recommendations?

From undertaking that exercise, you will see that promoting contact is delicately balanced and any contact recommendations should be based on what is in the child's best interests, considering their welfare and safeguarding needs, and not what the parent/carer wants.

It can be difficult to make these judgements, and therefore we have developed a tool to support you in making contact recommendations.

CONTACT RECOMMENDATIONS TOOL

Aim of the Contact Tool

This tool will support you in making professional judgements on contact, the time a child spends with their parent/carer.

As with safeguarding, there is no one size fits all. This tool has been created to help you break down the factors that you need to think about when making child-focused contact recommendations.

How to use the Contact Tool

When making recommendation on contact, you need to consider:

- *The safety of contact: should it be supervised, supported or unsupervised?*

- *The frequency of contact: how often should contact take place?*

- *The duration of contact: how long should contact be?*

- *Where contact should take place: such as in contact centre, in the community, in a relevant person's home?*

- *Who should attend contact?*

This tool is designed with question prompts aimed at helping you reach these recommendations. There are four sections to the tool to address each of these four factors: safety, frequency, duration and place. The tool resembles a traffic light system, to make this practical and tangible.

You do not have to tick each box; rather, this tool is a guide to develop your thinking of what you need to take account of when making contact recommendations.

(Continued)

(Continued)

Safety of contact

		Low risk	Medium risk	High risk
What are risks to contact?	What are the identified safeguarding risk of contact?	Low risk of harm being repeated in contact ☐	Medium risk of harm being repeated ☐	High risk of harm being repeated ☐
What are the child's experiences during contact?	Are contact risks the same as reasons for separation?	Parents are reliable in attending contact. ☐	Inconsistent contact attendance. ☐	Parents are unreliable in attending contact ☐
		Parents well presented in contact. ☐	Parents present inconsistently ☐	Parent's attendance in contact is poor i.e. under influence of substances ☐
		Parents responsive to child's needs ☐	Inconsistent responses to child ☐	Adult focused responses to contact. ☐
		Child has good experiences in contact; ☐	Child has inconsistent experiences in contact. ☐	Child experiences contact as neglectful and inattentive. ☐
		No flight risk i.e. no risk of abduction, child will be returned after contact ☐	Medium flight risk i.e. unreliability in sticking to contact times ☐	High flight risk i.e. risk of abduction/child not been returned after contact ☐
Who in the family can support contact?	Has a risk assessment been completed? Do they show insight into the risks?	Positive risks assessment; Family show insight and can act protectively ☐	Risk assessment identifies grey areas; family can protect with further work. ☐	Negative risk assessment; Family does not show insight and are not able to protect from further harm ☐
	Can they manage contact safely?	yes ☐	inconsistent ☐	No ☐

Key:

More indicators of high risk: contact should be supervised.

More indicators of medium risk: contact should be supported.

More indicators of low risk: contact can be unsupervised.

Frequency and duration of contact

		High	Medium	Low
What is the purpose of contact?	What are the child's care plans?	Is the care plan reunification?	Is the care plan long-term fostering?	Is the care plan Adoption?
What are the child's wishes and feelings? What does the child want to happen?	Do they want contact? Are they competent to make a choice?	yes	Ambivalent about contact	no
What are the child's needs?	How old is the child?	0–5 years	5–10 years	10–18 years
	What are their developmental needs? care-giving needs and how will contact impact these? These will be specific to each child but consider:	i.e. child needs to establish a care-giving relationship; or child needs regular/routine contact due to additional needs	Ambivalence in relationship; some additional care and support needs	i.e. child has high level of physical or emotional needs and can't manage high frequency of contact.
	Is the child able to manage the complex relationships?	Yes	With support	no
	What are the child's school/ afterschool commitments?	Low number of commitments	Medium number of activities	High number of activities

(Continued)

135

(Continued)

	High		Medium		Low	
What is the quality of parent/child relationship? How does the child experience their relationship with the parent?	Child feels accepted, loved, and has fun during contact. Their needs understood, met and responded to during contact	☐	Child's experiences are inconsistent	☐	Child feels rejected and neglected during contact	☐
Is the relationship established; what is the quality of attachment?	Good parent-child bond; Well established relationship	☐	Ambivalent; enmeshed parent-child bond	☐	Poor parent-child bond; relationships not established	☐
What is the impact of contact on the child? Is contact impacting on placement stability?	Child's behaviour is consistent after contact, no risk of placement breakdown.	☐	Sometimes the child's behaviours change after contact	☐	Child's behaviour reverts after contact putting placement at high risk of breakdown.	☐
	Contact supports child's placement	☐	Sometimes contact disrupts placement	☐	Contact diminishes progress child is making in placement	☐
What are the risks to contact? (refer to safety indicator, how do they apply to frequency indicators?) What are identified safeguarding risks?	Low risk of harm being repeated in contact	☐	Medium risk of harm being repeated.	☐	High risk of harm being repeated	☐
Are contact risks the same as reasons for separation?	Parents are reliable in attending contact	☐	Inconsistent contact attendance	☐	Parents are unreliable in attending contact	☐
	Parents well presented in contact	☐	Inconsistent presentation in contact	☐	Parent's attendance in contact is poor i.e. under influence of substances	☐
	Parents responsive to child's needs	☐	Inconsistent responses to child	☐	Adult-focused responses to contact	☐
	Child has good experiences in contact;		Child has inconsistent experiences in contact		Child experiences contact as neglectful and inattentive	
	No flight risk i.e. no risk of abduction, child will be returned after contact		Medium flight risk i.e. unreliability in sticking to contact times		High flight risk i.e. risk of abduction/child not been returned after contact	

	Quality of contact is good	Quality of contact is inconsistent	Quality of contact is poor
What is professional feedback?			
What is the distance between parent/carers and contact placement?	Close proximity (20–30 minutes)	Medium proximity (30–60 minutes)	Far distance 1 hours +

Key:

More indicators of high: higher frequency of contact should be considered; and long duration of contact;

More indicators of medium: medium level of contact should be consider

More indicators of low: the lower the frequency and lower duration of contact.

Place

Where contact takes place will be impacted upon by the assessment of the frequency, duration and safety of contact:

	Contact centre — Supervised	Community — Supported	Home environment — Unsupervised
What was the outcome of safety of contact?	☐	☐	☐
What are the realistic options for contact? — Do the parents have somewhere safe to take the child?	No ☐	Community-based options ☐	Yes ☐
What was the outcome of duration of contact?	Child can manage short period of contact? ☐	Child can manage longer period of contact? ☐	Child can manage pro-longer period of contact? ☐
Where does the child want to have contact? — Where does the child feel safe to have contact?	Contact centre ☐	Community ☐	Home environment ☐
What is the relationship between foster carer and parent? — Is there an established relationship to support contact relationships?	Foster carer/parent have not met; there are risks to this. ☐	Strained relationship; but can manage minimal contact ☐	Have a working relationship to support contact in relaxed environments. ☐

Now that we have given you a tool to assist in you reaching recommendations, let's look at how to apply this in practice.

ACTIVITY 6.7

Let us return to Activity 6.4 and Case Example 1 of Suzy and Joshua. Using our tool:

- *What contact recommendations would you make for Suzy and her mother?*
- *What contact recommendations would you make for Joshua and Zack?*

Here is some updated information for you to consider when thinking about the best contact recommendations:

- *During proceedings, Suzy was spending one night per week with Mary. Suzy has told the social worker she does not want to stay over anymore. She has been clear in her wishes and feelings that her mum does not understand her, and that she feels left out when she spends time with. She feels her mum prefers Joshua over her. Suzy feels conflicted about wanting a relationship with her mum but not having her emotional needs met in that relationship. The paternal grandfather reports that Suzy's behaviour changes after contact, she can become withdrawn and there can be a deterioration in behaviour leading up to contact.*

- *Zack is living in temporary accommodation and is working to save money to find his own, permanent accommodation.*

- *Zack is attending parenting courses and domestic abuse courses where his insight into safe parenting is increasing and changes to his behaviour are being observed.*

- *Zack is working with alcohol services. He has stopped using cocaine, which is consistent with Hair Strand Testing results. He uses cannabis 'now and again'.*

- *Joshua has had weekly, supervised contact during proceedings.*

Comment

Suzy's contact

From considering the information, work to rebuild the relationship between Mary and Suzy needs to be undertaken. Suzy experiences of contact are poor, but the risks are not such that it needs to be supervised. It can continue unsupervised. Suzy has expressed she does not want to stay over, and these come from real experiences. Contact is impacting on her, which supports the fact that contact should be less frequent. Suzy understands the significance of who Mary is to her and this is an important relationship to promote. It is safe for contact to take place either in the community or at Mary's house, which is a place Suzy is familiar with.

Appropriate contact recommendations will be for Suzy to see her mum monthly; this can take place at Mary's home address. Contact should be focused on rebuilding the relationship. Contact can be reviewed upon repartition work with a view to increasing contact to overnight stays.

Joshua's contact

Can this contact progress to unsupervised? In our assessment, yes. The risks are around domestic violence, which is reduced if parents are not in communication with each other and contact handovers are managed. Zack is child focused and responsive to Joshua's needs during contact. There are positive contact observations. Drug use is decreasing. The issue is where can contact take place? Recommendations can be made for this to take place in the community, unsupervised weekly, with a goal to Joshua spending overnights once his accommodation is secured.

REFLECTIVE QUESTION

The court has a duty to explore contact for all those important to the child. Therefore, what would you recommend about contact between Suzy and Joshua? Discuss with a colleague or your line manager.

Court Etiquette

Now that we have looked at what happens at court, we will briefly talk about court etiquette. How should you present yourself at court? Here are some tips and pointers:

- Dress professionally

- Upon arrival, sign in with the usher

- Find you solicitor/barrister

- Be courteous to parents or carers

- Outside of the court room, speak through your solicitor with regards to the issues agreed/disagreed. Be mindful of what you say to parties

- In court, stand when the judge or magistrates enter the room

- Sit behind your solicitor

- Be prepared: there may be information the court needs to access to make decisions, such as availability of placements, updates from agencies, etc.

Diversity and equality in Court work

The court has duties to ensure children and families have a fair trial. We will now look at some diversity and equality factors and accommodations a court makes to ensure fair and equal participation in care proceedings.

A parent with significant learning needs.	Cases where there are issues of domestic abuse and a fear of meeting the other parent.
What is a communicourt assessment? What is a Ground Rules hearing?	What adjustments can the court make?
Comment In cases where there are concerns around a parent's level of learning needs and capacity to give instructions, the court can direct a communicourt assessment. This is an assessment on the parent's communication skills, including their ability to instruct solicitors, understand and participate in hearings and communicate when giving evidence. It will also make recommendations on whether an intermediary is necessary. The comunicourt assessment gives recommendations on how to communicate with the vulnerable person, such as the language to be used and breaking information into smaller chunks, and any special measures which they need. Prior to the Final Hearing, there is a Ground Rules Hearing which discusses the findings from the report and how the hearing can be adapted to meet the vulnerable person's need, including appropriate communication and strategies to be used through the hearing. For example, when to take breaks, and whether questions will be agreed in advance. An intermediary will be present during the final hearing to support the vulnerable person.	*Comment* The court will be sensitive to these issues and can agree on arrangements such as parents entering and exiting through different entrances, sitting in different rooms of the court building, having screens up in court. These issues should be discussed through the parents' solicitors and asking the court to endorse these.

Remote ways of working and Court work

COVID-19 has impacted court work too where court hearings have been taking place remotely via video platforms. The President of The Family Division, Right Honourable Sir Andrew McFarlane, has written two reports entitled the Road

Ahead (09.06.2020 and 06.01.2021) on this issue. These papers give practice guidance on the legal issues of remote court hearing such as:

- Enabling the court to deal with cases justly, having regards to welfare issues

- Emphasis on ensuring lay persons are technically connected to the court process and understand what is occurring during the hearing

- COVID Case Management Checklist which gives guidance on narrowing the issues, the hearing format and optimising fairness of remote hearings

- Attendance at Court: it is for the judge to decide on a case-by-case basis whether one or all the parties should attend court. A hearing where some parties/professionals attend in person, and some remain remote is referred to as a hybrid hearing.

These are some of the legal implications of remote court hearings, but how does this impact on the social worker? An important part of court work is prehearing discussions. These are the discussions and negotiations before the court hearing. The purpose is to identify the key issues the court will need to make decisions on and narrow these down as far as possible. There is a risk this interface can be lost when working remotely. It is therefore important to make conscious efforts to speak to the necessary people before the court hearing.

Remote Court Etiquette

Earlier in this chapter, we talked about court etiquette. The courts are working remotely too, and hearing taking place via video links; and therefore what is remote court etiquette?

- It is still a formal process. Look smart and professional.

- Ensure you are in a place where you cannot be seen or overheard. It remains a private family matter.

- Have a separate line of communication with your solicitor so that you can communicate during the proceedings and provide instructions.

- Turn your camera on, unless advised to turn it off by the judge.

- Have an appropriate background to your camera.

Chapter summary

This chapter provides a detailed walk through the different stages of the court process and outlined the following areas:

- Public and Private Law

- Relevant orders in Public and Private Law

- The purpose and scope of the Legal Planning Meeting

- Your role in preparing for court

- Understanding the four stages of the court process: Issues and Applications, Case Management Hearing, Issues Resolution Hearing and Final Hearing.

- Equality and Diversity and remote working in court work.

YOUR LEARNING JOURNEY

This chapter has focused on court work. We have introduced you to the stages of the court process and given you a tool to use when making contact recommendation. How can you take this learning further? Stop and Think:

- *What have you learned about court work?*

- *How can you apply this in your practice?*

- *In this chapter, we have introduced you to some of the court orders you are most likely to come across. What are the some of the other orders a court can make. Research these in the Children Act 1989.*

- *What is a Secure Accommodation Order? What are the criteria for making this order and how is it different to the criteria of making other orders?*

- *A Position Statement is a legal document prepared by each party's legal representative before each hearing. What is this and how does it fit into the court process?*

- *As a social worker, after the Case Management hearing, you are required to continue working with the family through to the Final Hearing. The court process brings up powerful emotions and it is natural for families to experience feelings like anger and upset. How can you continue to build effective working relationships? Ask five different social workers in your organisation the skills they use and apply this in your practice.*

Chapter 7

Resilience in safeguarding children, young people and families

Chapter objectives

This chapter seeks to answer these questions:

- What is resilience?

- Why is resilience important?

- When do you need resilience?

- How can resilience be achieved?

Introduction

The role of the children and families social worker can be emotionally challenging, especially when working with parents/carers to prevent harm and risk to children and young people. Supporting hurting, confused, worried and angry children, as they work through their emotions and develop strategies to move forward, in spite of their past experiences, can be both distressing and satisfying for the social work practitioner. As stated in previous chapters, the involvement of other professionals is necessary, if we are to improve the lived experiences of children and young people subject of a safeguarding concern. Understanding the role of other professionals and navigating different expectations can represent yet another task to test the emotional resilience of the social work practitioner. Negotiating these competing demands requires resilient social work practitioners in the work environment.

Current literature suggests that social workers are one of the top professions to experience high levels of 'secondary trauma' (Quinn et al., 2018; Grant and Kinman., 2014; Bride et al., 2007). Secondary trauma or vicarious trauma is experienced when we observe, hear and understand a traumatic event from the child's perspective (Ludick and Figley, 2016). Figley (1995: 07) defines secondary trauma as:

> The natural consequent behaviours resulting from knowledge about a traumatising event experienced by a significant other. It is the stress resulting from wanting to help a traumatised or suffering person.

Therefore, as we engage and build relationships with children and families it is inevitable that we feel the effects of the trauma experienced by others. However, we know that when social workers are enabled to explore their own feelings, through the use of effective supervision, the impact of secondary trauma can be significantly reduced. This chapter will consider what is resilience. Consideration will also be given to why achieving a state of wellness and well-being is important for the social work practitioner. To remain well, resilient and able to avoid the risk of secondary trauma, it is imperative for social workers to develop strategies to protect and enhance their resilience and general well-being at work. We will discuss and outline a range of strategies that can support you in your journey of becoming a resilient social work practitioner.

What is resilience?

According to Ungar (2010: 425), the construct of resilience can be defined as the following:

> In the context of exposure to significant adversity, resilience is both the capacity of the individual to navigate their way to the psychological, social, cultural and physical resources that sustain their wellbeing, and their capacity individually and collectively to negotiate for these resources to be provided in culturally meaningful ways.

> (Source: https://resilienceresearch.org/about-resilience/.
> (Accessed March 2020))

Resilience is a response to adversity and challenge, by the individual in a given situation and environment. It is the interaction between the individual and their environment, where attempts are made to navigate and negotiate the resources required to sustain their well-being. Literature on well-being suggest that well-being includes a state of happiness, enjoyment and personal growth and fulfilment (Marmot, 2004). For the social work practitioner, well-being will be informed by their own personality type and attributes. The extant literature on resilience has indicated that resilient social workers possess the following attributes (Grant and Kinman, 2020):

The attributes outlined in Table 7.1 will be of benefit to a practitioner working with children and young people feeling pain and distress caused by a traumatic life event. As part of the intervention stage, a key role of the social worker is to encourage children and young people to utilise the time and space provided to talk about their past experiences. For the child and young person it is imperative they are allowed the necessary time to respond and release the emotions associated with their trauma safely and without judgement. In many cases, social workers act as a funnel

Table 7.1   Attributes of resilience in social workers based on literature

- Self-efficacy and self-esteem.
- Enthusiasm, optimism and hope.
- Openness to experience.
- A positive self-concept and a strong sense of identity.
- An internal locus of control (where an individual attributes success to their own efforts and abilities) and a high degree of autonomy.
- Self-awareness and emotional literacy.
- Self-compassion and the ability to prioritise self-care.
- Critical thinking skills.
- The ability to set appropriate boundaries.
- Well-developed social skills and the social confidence to develop effective relationships with people from different backgrounds.
- Flexibility and adaptability, drawing on a wide range of coping strategies and creative problem-solving skills.
- The ability to recognise and draw on one's unique pattern of internal and external resources.
- The ability to identify and draw on sources of support.
- Persistence in the face of challenges, setbacks and adversity.
- A sense of purpose and the ability to derive a sense of meaning from difficulties and challenges.
- The ability to learn from experience.
- An orientation towards the future.
- A sense of humour.

Source: Grant and Kinman (2020) https://local.gov.uk/sites/default/files/documents/workforce%20-%20wellbeing%20social%20care%20-%20Community%20Care%20Inform%20emotional%20resilience%20guide.pdf.

for the pain of the child and young person, and so must themselves be able to release this pain (see Figure 7.1). For the child and young person, the ability to release the pain associated with their past will be influenced by the extent to which the social worker is understanding, offers both time and space for the child to explore their own emotions. Children and young people need to know that the social worker is also emotionally invested and that they care, and this can only be achieved when there is a foundation of relationship-based social work. Whilst there is no one definition of relationship-based social work, it is acknowledged there are central ingredients. Firstly, the relationship between the social worker and the service user is the foundation of effective practice. Trevithick (2012: 13) reminds us this should be 'at the heart of social work'. The application of relationship-based social work requires the building block of effective communication. We must be sensitive and intentional in how we communicate during periods of trauma. At each stage the social worker will have had to demonstrate resilience.

Why is resilience important?

The absence of resilience for the social worker has many consequences ranging from emotional exhaustion to burnout. According to Pines and Maslach (1978), burnout occurs when social workers experience lethargy, negativity and cynicism which is evidenced over time and leads to exhaustion and the inability to cope and perform tasks in a safe way (Maslach, 2017). Burnout has an impact on the social

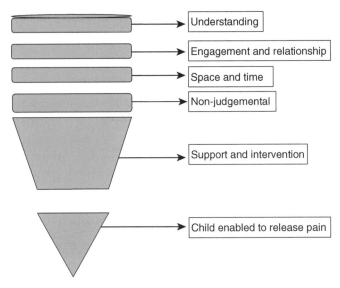

Figure 7.1   The emotional funnel in social work practice

work practitioner, client, other professionals and the wider social work team. For example, research by McFadden (2015) measured burnout among UK Social Workers. The findings suggest that the risk of becoming emotionally hardened to service users is increased by poor supervision.

ACTIVITY 7.1

Stop and think

Resilience is needed to guard against secondary trauma and burnout. Read the example below and then consider the following questions.

As a newly qualified social worker, I observed an interview with an experienced colleague where a mother told us she was using cocaine daily, was being hit and beaten by her partner regularly (she attended the interview with a bruised eye) and did not know if she really wanted to keep the baby with whom she was pregnant with. Having had a sheltered upbringing, I remember listening to what this mother was telling us and having to consciously stop my eyes from popping out of my head. This mother was telling me experiences she was having which I had only read about and not yet come across. It made them real. I had to reflect on how I could develop resilience to come to terms that hurt and pain is a real experience for some people, and to then hold interviews and conversations about these risk factors to establish the level of risk and harm to a child.

- *How will it impact upon you, hearing about safeguarding risk factors for the first time? Make a list of words that describe your emotions.*

- *How do you remain empathetic and person centred when you have heard the same or similar experience repeatedly?*

Comment

It is natural to feel emotions such as hurt, pain, discomfort, disbelief, upset, anger and frustration when hearing about safeguarding concerns for the first time. When interviewing children and families, we need to manage our own feelings to properly support and assess the family situation. Being prepared for these likely scenarios, such as doing the above activity, will develop your resilience and ability to respond sensitively to children and families when undertaking safeguarding work.

If a social worker does not have resilience, there is a risk of safeguarding practice becoming too routine and losing sight of the individual child and family, and the individual impact of their experiences. This point was made apparent to me when watching the responses of a mother during a judgement at the conclusion of care proceedings. It was a positive outcome, and the child was being returned to the mother's care as she had made and sustained changes to her parenting responses. However, as the honourable judge delivered his judgement and addressed each of the concerns which had caused the child significant harm, such as associating with unsafe and risky individuals and purposeful neglect, this mother showed genuine upset and distress, highlighting to me the person behind the harm. This is not to detract from the importance of assessment and harm identification which is crucial to a safeguarding role. Rather, it is to highlight that as experienced professionals we need to continue to approach each case with the same level of empathy, and not 'write people off' because we think we have heard the same story before. We need to remember these are real experiences happening to real people and not let the terms 'mental health', 'domestic violence', 'drug use' and 'sexual harm' become routine words and phrases which roll off our tongues. We need resilience to guard against becoming complacent and lacking empathy. We need to approach each case with empathy, a fresh pair of eyes, a new perspective and a drive to motivate change for the benefit of the child, young person and their family.

When do you need resilience?

To answer this question, it is important to remind ourselves of the purposes of safeguarding.

Social work and carrying out safeguarding responsibilities is a complex and demanding profession. The most common misconception is that social workers 'take children away'. This is something that is heard all the time when practicing as a social worker. The purpose of social work is quite the opposite. As stated in previous chapters, essential to social work practice is ensuring children are safe and happy, and every effort to achieve this by keeping a child in their family network is made. It is only in extreme cases where children cannot be kept safe by their parents/carers, and it is identified that they are at risk of suffering significant harm, that a local authority makes an application to the court to request consideration is given to where the child should live in the short and long term. This is the court's decision, and whilst informed by the social worker's report and recommendation, it is not the social worker's final decision. The social worker is fulfilling statutory responsibilities by alerting the state of the safeguarding risks. The social worker then has responsibilities for implementing the decisions the court makes.

In this safeguarding role, as professionals, we come across harrowing experiences. We see suffering, sadness and acts which go against the grain of humanness. We are not in a movie where effects are dramatised and you can console yourself that it is fiction, it is made up, it did not really happen. What we come across is real-life experiences, events that happened, incidents that have caused suffering, hurt and harm. In trying to effect change, we deal with parents who often have suffered their own adverse experiences in a cycle of abuse, we deal with conflict, with parents who are angry or cannot see the need to do something differently. These are the realities of safeguarding children and young people. As professionals we need to be resilient, we need to be strong to manage these challenges as they become our day-to-day tasks.

Resilience is a key social work skill and foundational to longevity in the profession. Resilience is needed as a student social worker, as a newly qualified social worker, as an experienced worker, and as a social work manager and senior manager. What we need resilience for changes as we learn, grow, develop and become experienced professionals. It will also be impacted by the experiences, values and beliefs we bring individually to our professional roles. For example, an acrimonious relationship break-up in your personal life could impact on your responses to cases where domestic abuse is a concern. Or undergoing training on child exploitation could make you more resilient in managing a case with this safeguarding concern.

How can resilience be achieved?

We will now look at how you can build resilience in your practice through the following activity.

ACTIVITY **7.2**

Stop and think

Consider these likely scenarios that you will come across when safeguarding children and young people. What do you think your response will be? How can you develop resilience to manage these scenarios?

- *Which safeguarding risk factors are you comfortable hearing about and assessing? Which ones 'hit too close to the bone' and need further self-reflection?*

- *How do you feel about having to remove a child from a parent/carer, and the distress this may cause?*

- *How will you respond when a parent shouts aggressively at you or calls you names?*

- *How will you respond when a complaint is made about you?*

As a social worker, or professional in a safeguarding role, we must be equipped and able to manage these core issues in safeguarding children and young people. Human nature is complex and coming across these scenarios will impact on different people differently. Some key tips for achieving resilience are the following:

- *Being child focused:* think about what you know about the day-to-day experience for the child. Are your actions going to make a positive difference for this child, even if the child cannot understand or appreciate it at the point of intervention? Remember, children are children, and they need adults to make safe decisions for them.

- *Having a clear evidence base with defensible decisions:* know the reasons for your actions, ensure there is an evidence base to support them and be confident in following through with them.

- *Knowing the legal frameworks:* all safeguarding practice is guided by statutory frameworks. Knowing the remit of these in safeguarding decision-making can negate worry and give assurances for interventions.

- *Remaining professional:* embed social work and workplace codes of practice into your role so you can be satisfied you carried out all social work tasks professionally, ethically and under national and local frameworks.

- *Using Supervision Effectively:* use supervision to talk through your professional experiences and how they have made you feel.

Does a career in social work have a 'sell by date'?

As aforementioned, what we need is resilience for changes as we learn, grow, develop and become experienced professionals. The reflective questions outlined in Activity 6.2 are perhaps more common scenarios for which someone at the start of their career will need resilience in. The more experienced we become as professionals, the more confident we become in our professional roles and responsibilities and the better we get at managing these issues. In the middle to the end of social work careers we need resilience to stay in the profession. There is a risk of becoming professionally exhausted or burnt out from high caseloads and the demands of the job. A report on the social work profession For Social Work England (YouGov, 2020) summarises that the most common reason for people to leave social work is the high workload (39%), followed by poor mental or physical health (32%) and poor work–life balance (29%). There is also a risk of becoming disillusioned when all we see on a day-to-day basis is harm and suffering. We need to develop resilience to stay in the profession.

Strategies for resilience

We now turn our attention to strategies for achieving and maintaining resilience.

Using supervision effectively

The functions of supervision are to ensure that you as a social worker are well and able to carry out your job to meet the needs of the service. A social work manager is responsible for checking on your well-being, that you are equipped and have the learning and training to carry out your role, and that you are safeguarding and improving the outcomes for children and young people. Therefore, it is important that supervision is prioritised and properly prepared for. Talk openly in supervision about what is going well and what, if anything, you are finding difficult. Being transparent allows the correct support, guidance and mentoring to be put in place. Use supervision to talk through cases and have reflective conversations on what you did, and what you could have done differently. Use supervision to identify training which can meet gaps in your learning and development. All this will support resilience.

We have developed a well-being index that can be used in your supervision sessions to explore your well-being and the areas you might require support with.

WELL-BEING INDEX TOOL

Aim of the Well-being Index Tool

This tool will support you to explore your current well-being and help to promote your resilience at work.

Well-being is an individual experience and there is no one size fits all. Your well-being appraisal will help you to identify what matters to your well-being and the support required. This tool has been created to help you break down the factors that you need to think about when identifying strategies to support your well-being with your line manager.

How to use the Well-being Index Tool

When engaging in a discussion about your well-being, you should think about:

- *The strengths you have that support your well-being: For example, I am an effective communicator.*

- *Access to informal support networks: How often does this happen?*

- *The workload pressure points: What are they? How long will this last for?*

- *The learning needs required to support your growth and development at work: such as a course on relaxation techniques or observing an experienced colleague chair a challenging meeting.*

- *The impact of others (team members, service user and other professionals: explore the effects and how response required).*

- *Inclusivity and Respect: examples of how behaviours, attitudes and practices at work create an environment of respect and inclusion.*

There are six factors in the well-being index tool and these are: strengths, support, workload pressure point, learning needs, impact of others and

---

inclusivity and respect. The tool uses a scale (0–5) to help you rate each area, and to make a well-being plan with your line manager.

This tool is a guide to develop your thinking about what you need to support your well-being at work when talking with your manager.

Strengths

Reflect on and record your current strengths at work.	**Well-being Scale** On a scale of 0–5, how would you rate this aspect? 5 = Experiencing positive (high level) of well-being 0 = Experiencing negative (low) well-being in this area
	0 5
Well-being action plan 1. Xxxxxxxxxx 2. Xxxxxxxxxx 3. xxxxxxxxxxx	

Support networks

Reflect on and record your current informal support networks at work.	**Well-being Scale** On a scale of 0–5, how would you rate this aspect? 5 = Experiencing positive (high level) of well-being 0 = Experiencing negative (low) well-being in this area
	0 5
Well-being action plan 1. Xxxxxxxxxx 2. Xxxxxxxxxx 3. xxxxxxxxxxx	

Workload pressure points

Reflect on and record your current workload pressure points at work.	**Well-being Scale** On a scale of 0–5, how would you rate this aspect? 5 = Experiencing positive (high level) of well-being 0 = Experiencing negative (low) well-being in this area
	0 5
Well-being action plan 1. Xxxxxxxxxx 2. Xxxxxxxxxx 3. xxxxxxxxxxx	

(Continued)

(Continued)

Learning needs

Reflect on and record your current learning needs at work.	Well-being Scale On a scale of 0–5, how would you rate this aspect? 5 = Experiencing positive (high level) of well-being 0 = Experiencing negative (low) well-being in this area
	0 5

Well-being action plan
1. Xxxxxxxxxx
2. Xxxxxxxxxx
3. xxxxxxxxxxx

Impact of others (team members, service user and other professionals)

Reflect on and record the effects of others at work.	Well-being Scale On a scale of 0–5, how would you rate aspect? 5 = Experiencing positive (high level) of well-being 0 = Experiencing negative (low) well-being in this area
	0 5

Well-being action plan.
1. Xxxxxxxxxx
2. Xxxxxxxxxx
3. Xxxxxxxxxxx
4. Xxxxxxxxxxx
5. xxxxxxxxxxx

Inclusivity and respect

Reflect on and record your current experiences of inclusivity and respect at work.	Well-being Scale On a scale of 0–5, how would you rate aspect? 5 = Experiencing positive (high level) of well-being 0 = Experiencing negative (low) well-being in this area
	0 5

Well-being action plan.
1. Xxxxxxxxxx
2. Xxxxxxxxxx
3. Xxxxxxxxxxx
4. xxxxxxxxxxxx

Now that we have introduced you to our well-being index tool, let us consider the following case example to see how you can use it in your discussions with your line manager.

CASE STUDY

You have completed an assessment, and receive the following email response from the parent:

please do not contact me again. I am currently seeking legal advice and escalating your slanderous and unsubstantiated report with the ombudsman.

- *How does this make you feel?*

- *What well-being index factor does it relate to?*

- *What if anything can be included in your well-being plan?*

Comment

The tone of this email is harsh and threatening. It is natural for it to make you feel upset, anxious, worried and to have a loss of confidence. This is an example of the effects that others have on you. It is also an example of the importance of reports having evidence-based and defensible decisions-making, as discussed in Chapter 3. It may be that the report was substantiated, and it would be important to reflect on this in your discussions with your manager. A possible well-being action plan could be to go on a training course around dealing with conflict or report writing as a refresher.

Upskilling

As social workers and professionals in a safeguarding role, we have a professional responsibility to ensure we meet requirements for Continuous Professional Development (CPD). This is regulated through the workplace and Social Work England. Keeping up-to-date with social work issues equips us with the skills, knowledge and behaviours for effective safeguarding practice. The information empowers us to be resilient and have the skillset to approach safeguarding with confidence. Training is often the first thing to be missed when caseloads are high, yet critical to keeping up resilience. Training and learning should always be prioritised.

Managing high caseloads

High caseloads are often the most cited reason for social workers leaving the profession or becoming burnt out. Here are some tips for managing high caseloads.

Case plans

When a case is allocated, take the time to plan. This allows you to think about the initial issues and risks which have been identified in the case, and to think about your approach to the case: what needs to happen to progress the case and achieve positive outcomes, and to plan for timescales, by when does this needs to take place? This will give a clear idea of what needs to be done and by when. Work backwards and block out time in your diary for writing the assessment, for interviews, telephone calls etc. Some local authorities/organisations will have case plans in place.

We have devised some questions to support your approach to a case and enable you to manage a case load effectively. When you are allocated a case, read the information in the referral, and spend time thinking about the following:

What are the identified issues: the risks and strengths?

Risks:

Strengths:

Who are the agencies involved?

Who is in the family?

What are their diversity factors that need to be considered?

What are your working hypotheses of what is going on for the family?

What theory, research and assessment tools will support your assessment of the family?

What information is missing?

Sharing information: Which agencies do you need to get information from? And by when?

Who do you need to interview? And by when?

How long do you need to write the report?

Who needs to read the report before it is signed off?

By when must the report be completed?

Be organised and have effective diary management

Put everything in your diary however big or small and stick to it as far as possible. There are times when other work needs to be prioritised, that is part of the job. However, make sure that whatever you are rearranging gets rescheduled back in your work diary. It is also helpful to set some realistic tasks for each day or week and work to achieve those.

Prioritise work effectively

Factors to consider when prioritising work include the following:

- The level of risk: for example, what framework is the case being managed under, Child in Need (CIN), child protection or care proceedings. Responding to high-risk cases should be prioritised.

- The gravitas of deadlines. Who is the deadline for and what is the impact if it is not met?

- The complexity of the family situation, including complex needs and challenging parents.

- When unsure, always seek guidance from your manager.

We will now look at how to prioritise work in the following case examples.

CASE STUDY

Consider these two case scenarios which you are likely to come across. Which piece of work should be prioritised in each scenario?

Scenario 1

Your work commitments scheduled in your diary for Tuesday are to start writing a Children and Family Assessment that is due the following week and undertake a

(Continued)

CASE STUDY continued

home visit to progress an assessment on a different family. Two hours before your home visit, a safeguarding referral is received for another child on your caseload, raising concerns that the school have observed bruising on the child in areas that are unlikely to get bruises.

Scenario 2

Your work commitments scheduled in your diary for Thursday are to write a Court Statement that is due for filing the next day. Midmorning, a safeguarding referral is received for another child on your caseload, raising concerns that the school have observed bruising on the child in areas that are unlikely to get bruises.

- What piece of work should be prioritised in Scenario 1 and Scenario 2?

- What are the factors which influence your decision-making on which work should be prioritised?

Comment

In Scenario 1, responding to the safeguarding referral should be prioritised as the other pieces of work are important but non-urgent. In Scenario 2, both pieces of work are high risk and important. The court report should be prioritised as this is the highest authority requesting the work. The safeguarding referral can be responded to by the team manager, supported by duty.

Let's consider one more scenario.

CASE STUDY

Scenario 3

Your work commitments on Monday are a Child in Need meeting. This is for a family who have raised complaints to the range of the services involved with the family. They feel there is no joined up working between agencies. It has been difficult finding a date which all the involved professionals can attend. This Child in Need meeting has been agreed four weeks in advance. When you arrive at work on Monday morning, another child on your case load has been placed in emergency accommodation over the weekend. It is not local to his school, he is refusing to go in taxi, the foster carer does not drive and is unable to take him.

Reflective question

- *What should you prioritise, attending the Child in Need meeting or taking the child to school?*

Comment

There are complexities identified for the family whom the CIN meeting is scheduled for. The task of taking the child to school can be picked up by another social worker who knows him.

Use technology to your advantage

This may be limited by the resources made available by your employer. Become familiar with the apps available and use them for streamlining recording.

As social workers we often go above and beyond our duty. Work to what is reasonable and expected and do not be shy of raising it with managers when you feel your workload is getting too much. If you do not tell them, they will not know.

A personal well-being plan

We talk about care plans for the children and families we work with. We think carefully about what needs to be achieved to improve things for them. What about your own care and well-being plan? What are the thing things that are important to you that let you escape the demands of the job to keep you feeling uplifted and energised? We need to look after ourselves and ensure we are in a good place to carry out the job we do. Set aside some 'me time' each week.

Have a break

Safeguarding children and young people is complex, challenging and demanding. We are highly skilled professionals with specialist training. It may be impractical to 'take a break' as such. For many of us this is where we have invested years of training and learning and is our primary source of income. However, there is something to be said for change and variety. There are a range of roles in which social work skills can be used in. Local authorities divide their safeguarding functions into different teams. For example, there is the 'front door service', which screens and triages all referrals, often referred to as Multi Agency Safeguarding Hub; Assessment teams, which carry out short-term work; family safeguarding teams, which carry out long-term work; Children Looked After teams, which ensure children's needs are being met when the local authority is a corporate parent; fostering and adoption teams, which assess and match children to carers;

disabled children teams, which provide support and safeguarding services to children with additional needs; and independent reviewing teams. Cafcass is the largest employer of social workers in England and offers a safeguarding service to children and families who are going through the family courts in either private law or public law proceedings. There are social work roles in some charities. The different areas of social work will provide different pressures and different releases. When you feel you are reaching burnout, it can be invigorating and energising to change your area of social work practice.

Annual leave

Taking regular annual leave can help maintain your resilience. Knowing you only have, for example, six weeks until your next holiday, breaks the job down into bite-sized and manageable chunks.

Diversity and equality and resilience and well-being

When considering diversity and equality alongside resilience and well-being, we refer you to the Well-being Index that we introduced you to earlier in this chapter. What are your diversity and equality needs, and are they being respected and included in the workplace? This should be a factor discussed regularly in supervision.

Remote ways of working and resilience and well-being

As stated in previous chapters, social workers are working more remotely due to the impact of COVID-19. This can feel isolating and there is not the immediate team support for encouragement or debrief when we come across challenging situations. Working remotely also means there is the potential for poor work–life boundaries, and it can feel like 'we are living at work'. A survey completed by Turner (2020) looking at the impact of coronavirus identified that 75% of social workers are feeling more negative about their work life and that factors such as increasing caseloads, complexity of cases and increased level of needs among people we support are contributing factors. These statistics emphasise that the job is challenging, and we need to look after ourselves. We need to do this job together. Therefore, it is important to find ways to stay connected and feel supported when working remotely.

REFLECTIVE QUESTION

- *How can you continue to access support from your manager and team when working remotely?*

Comment

The answer to this will depend on the resources made available by your team and employer. Some tips for staying connected include the following:

- Be linked with a mentor/buddy who you can call throughout the working day/ week for guidance and support.

- Have regular team check-ins on a video platform.

- Do not be shy to discuss issues with your manager. They are there to support you.

Hampshire County Council developed a Well-being Hub during the coronavirus pandemic. This provides a good case study for how to support employee well-being. Information can be found on the Social Work England YouTube Channel, Speaker's corner, Monday, Social Work Week 2021 (https://youtu.be/mcNcp1ow8XQ, accessed 26 May 2021). The Well-being Hub offered online resources, 1-2-1 sessions and group reflective sessions to support social workers to channel well-being questions, practice challenges or managing things such as studies, technology, working from home. They did this using different activities, such as:

- Kubler Ross Model, supporting social workers to work through their emotions and experiences and understanding that others are going through the same.

- Control and influence circle, supporting social workers to talk through their frustrations and to think about what they can control, what is out of control and what they should focus on.

- Reflective jar—reflect on strengths and good experiences.

We will end this section with a reflective question.

- What can you take away from this case study to improve your resilience and well-being in a remote way of working? Talk this through with your line manager.

Chapter summary

- Resilience is how we respond to adversity and challenge.

- Resilience is needed by social workers because we come across hurt, pain and suffering in our safeguarding roles.

- Our well-being index sets out six factors important to your well-being which should be discussed with your manager. These are: strengths, support, workload pressure point, learning needs, impact of others and inclusivity and respect.

- Strategies for resilience.

YOUR LEARNING JOURNEY

In this chapter we have looked at well-being and resilience. Stop and Think:

- *From reading this chapter, what have you learned about well-being and resilience?*
- *What can you do to promote your resilience and well-being?*
- *Write your own personal well-being plan.*
- *Mind, a mental health charity offers five ways to well-being which include the following:*
  - *Connect*
  - *Be active*
  - *Take notice*
  - *Learn*
  - *Give*

Look these up at https://www.mind.org.uk/workplace/mental-health-at-work/taking-care-of-yourself/five-ways-to-wellbeing/

- *How can you incorporate this in your personal and work life?*

We will leave you with a concluding comment:

When safeguarding is a key responsibility of your job, and it is what you do daily, it is easy to forget that it is only a small number of the population who perpetrate or experience harm.

Out of the 12 million children living in England, just over 400,000 (3%) are in the social care system at any one time *(Ofsted, 2021).*

Chapter 8
Checklists for effective practice

Chapter objectives

This chapter will seek to answer the following questions:

- What are the expectations of the social worker and key actions required when assessing children and families under Child in Need Frameworks?

- What are the expectations of the social worker and key actions required when assessing children and families under Child Protection Frameworks?

- What are the expectations of the social worker and key actions required when assessing children and families under Public Law Outline and Care Proceedings?

- What are the expectations of the social worker and key actions required when assessing children and families under Child Looked After Frameworks?

Introduction

This chapter will aim to provide the social worker with a guide to what actions need to be undertaken and under what timescales when carrying out safeguarding assessments under differing frameworks including Child in Need (CIN), Child Protection, Public Law Outline and Care Proceedings and Child Looked After frameworks.

It will provide a quick reference through checklists and case examples to aid the practitioner's understanding of the actions required and expectations of the social worker's role.

Child in Need: key social work actions

The *Framework for the assessment of children in need and their families* (Department of Health et al., 2000) is a tool to help social workers to understand the lived experiences of the child/young person at home within their families and their wider community. The framework is primarily for local authorities (Children Services) who have the lead responsibility for assessing children in need, including children who may be suffering or are suffering significant harm. All agencies have a duty under Section 27 of the Children Act 1989 to assist the social worker in contributing and support the social worker undertaking the assessment. This expectation is further reinforced in the *Working Together to Safeguard Children* (2018) guidance.

It is recognised that many families receive support from friends, families and services in the community and are not likely to require additional support. Department of Health, Department of Education and Employment, Home Office (2000) is a useful tool when considering families that may require additional support to improve the future well-being of the child. For example, this means that in some circumstances, a decision will be made by the parent or carer to seek additional support or alternatively is referred for targeted support from education, children services, health, family support, mental health services and alcohol/drug support services.

We will turn our attention to the following case example to explain the social worker roles and responsibilities in more detail.

CASE STUDY

The initial concern raised by Bright Sparks, nursery manager, was that June Smith (Mother, aged twenty-four) had hit Ana (Daughter, aged three) two times across the back of her legs and face when dropping her off at the Nursery in January 2020. This was verified by several witnesses (mothers) who were dropping off their children at the time and by June who commented she had been under pressure lately and sometimes hits Ana.

Reflective question

Is this a Child in Need of family support or other intervention?

Comment

To determine if this is a CIN as defined within the Children Act 1989, ask yourself what is likely to happen to the child's health and development without a service or intervention. Also, reflect on how the services will improve the health and development of the child/young person.

Remember the criteria (section 17(10)) of the Children Act 1989 for a Child in Need is:

1. *He is unlikely to achieve or maintain or to have the opportunity of achieving or maintaining a reasonable standard of health or development without the provision for him or services by a local authority.*

2. *His health or development is likely to be significantly impaired, or further impaired, without the provision for him or such services; or*

3. *He is disabled (A child is defined as disabled 'if he is blind, deaf or dumb or suffers from a mental disorder of any kind) or is substantially and permanently*

handicapped by illness, injury or congenital or other such disability as may be prescribed (s17(11)).

How to assess children and families under Child in Need

Here are some tips for effective practice when carrying out assessments. The above case example is referred to demonstrate how to apply these tips into practice.

1. *Clarify the source of the referral and reasons.* For example, check details with the nursery manager and information held on Children Services records. Always verify the child's details.

2. *Acquisition of Information.* Who do you need to interview? Talk with Ana, nursery staff, mother and health visitor (if available).

3. *Exploring facts and feelings.* For example, explain June's and Ana's account and feelings of the incident.

4. *Give meaning to the situation from different perspectives.* For example, what do we know about Ana's background?

5. *Produce an analysis of the needs of the child and parenting capacity.* Refer back to our assessment and decision-making tool that was described in Chapter 3. Do other children live in the household? What is the role of the father? Is there a current partner within the household?

Once you have determined this is a CIN, CIN processes must be followed including formulating a CIN plan, reviewing the child's plan through regular CIN meetings and carrying out regular CIN visits.

Child in Need plan

A CIN plan sets out the identified risks to the child or young person, the identified services to reduce/eliminate the risk and the expectations of the family and pro-fessionals to improve outcomes for the child and young person, all of which are set to timescales (see Chapter 5).

Child in Need meeting

A CIN meeting is usually chaired by the social worker; however, if there are complex issues, at times it may be chaired by the team manager. A CIN meeting is attended by the professionals involved with the child. The focus of the meeting is to discuss the services required to improve the outcomes for the child or young person and review the impact of them and progress of the CIN plan (see Chapter 5). CIN meetings should take place six times weekly, and this should be more regular, every four weeks, if there are higher levels of concerns. During supervision, you should discuss risks with your manager and agree on the frequency of CIN meetings.

If a child is open due to their disability and receiving a care package that is meeting assessed need, and there are no identified safeguarding concerns, CIN meetings can be less frequent, such as three to six times monthly. Again, this frequency should be agreed with your manager and in line with local and national policy.

Child in Need visit

CIN visits should take place four to six times weekly. The purpose is to obtain the child's or young person's updated wishes and feelings, and make observations of the home environment and family relationships.

Child Protection: key social work actions

We will now consider the key actions required when assessing children and families under Child Protection Frameworks, using the following case example.

CASE STUDY

Case A

Family composition

Mum: Sally, 39

Dad: Doug, 30

Faye, 12

Luke, 9

Julie, 7

Sally has driven to a family member's party with all three children in her cousin's car. Doug decided to drive the family car later that evening and meet Sally and their children at the family function. Sally and Doug proceeded to drink, and both were under the influence of alcohol. At the end of the party (just after midnight), Doug and Sally took the decision to drive home with all the children in their car. Unfortunately, there was a car accident, resulting in the car turning over and the eldest child (Faye) was hospitalised due to suffering a head injury and was put into a medically induced coma. Doug and Sally were remorseful and distraught by the incident. The police were called, and the parents were arrested for both being under the influence of alcohol. The children were placed in foster care under a S20 agreement on a temporary basis. Parental aunt stepped in to look after Luke and Julie whilst Faye recovered in the hospital.

Reflective question

*   *Is this a child protection case?*

Comment

This case was considered under the child protection framework due to the fact both parents knowingly drove a car under the influence of alcohol, leading to their eldest child suffering a head injury.

Now that it has been assessed that the case should be managed under the child protection framework, let's look at the key actions required to reach this decision, and the ongoing social work tasks to improve outcomes for the children. These are as follows:

- Strategy discussion

- Complete an initial assessment

- Child protection conference

- Core group meetings to monitor the child protection plan

- Statutory child protection visits, to visit the child at home

Strategy discussion

The purpose of the strategy meeting is for each agency attending to share information on the child and family, to make a joint assessment on the presenting risk and to make decisions on the next steps, which could include either:

- To undertake enquiries under S47 of the Children Act 1989 and to reconvene for a Review Strategy Discussion, such as when more information is required.

- To undertake enquiries under S47 of The Children Act 1989 and to proceed to a Child Protection Conference, such as when the risk identified is high.

- Whether there should be a single agency or joint investigation. For example, will the police be investigating any crime (joint investigation)?

The legal guidance states that strategy meetings should be held within forty-eight hours of a safeguarding concern being raised, but there are examples of this occurring within twenty-four hours, for example, when there are unexplained injuries on the child and there is a need to obtain timely medical evidence, through a child protection medical. A child protection medical is a medical assessment of the child undertaken by a paediatrician who is trained in safeguarding. The purpose of a child protection medical is to determine if the injury caused to the child is accidental or non-accidental. A child protection medical can only progress if this is an agreed action from a strategy discussion.

The strategy meeting should be attended at a minimum by the social worker, social work manager, police and health representatives. Any professional involved with the child should be invited to attend too, such as the safeguarding lead from the children's school, health visitor, etc. However, on occasions, the strategy meeting can be held with only the police and social work manager if an urgent outcome is required, as in the example cited when a decision needs to be made on whether to progress with a child protection medical, or where there are immediate risks about the child going home.

A strategy discussion is chaired by the Team Manager or Service Manager.

Child protection conference

The child protection conference is usually held within ten days of the strategy discussion. The purpose of the conference is to discuss the risk factors, the protective factors and any grey areas. The child protection conference will determine if the child is likely to suffer or has suffered significant harm. A decision will be made whether a child should be made subject to a child protection plan and agree under which category (neglect, emotional harm, physical harm or sexual harm) they should be registered.

A child protection conference is attended by agencies relevant to the child. This usually includes the conference chair, parents, the child (where appropriate), the social worker and their manager, police, health, education as well as other professionals actively working with the family, such as domestic abuse services, housing, midwife, health visitor, alcohol services, mental health worker, etc. For a child protection conference to go ahead, it must be quorant. This means a minimum of three professional disciplines are required to attend the conference.

A child protection conference is chaired by the Child Protection Chair, who is independent of the social work team. A child protection chair must not have any operational or line management responsibility for the case. This allows objectivity and fairness to the process. The child protection chair has responsibilities to facilitate equal family and professional participation and to uphold anti-discriminatory values during the meeting.

The child protection plan, the actions to improve outcomes for the child, is agreed at the child protection conference. The conference chair will also agree the members of the core group, which is the mechanism for monitoring the child protection plan.

Core group meeting

Core group meetings are held every four to six weeks to monitor the care plan and prevent drift and delay for the child/young person. The members of the core group are typically those who are providing a service to the child or young person such as the social worker, school nurse, teacher or any specialist service. The members of the core group can be fluid. For example, a school nurse may initially attend the core group; however, if there is an assessment that the child's health needs are being met, it is disproportionate for the school nurse to continue attending the core group meetings.

Statutory child protection visits

Child Protection visits should take place every four weeks by the social worker. This can vary if there is a need for closer monitoring. You should see the child's bedroom and see them alone when it is appropriate to do so. Ensure your visits address the identified safeguarding concerns. For example, if the concerns have been about the children being regularly hungry, then make sure you have conversations with the parents/carer and children about this, and observe mealtimes.

REFLECTIVE QUESTIONS

Now that the child protection processes have been explained, return to case example A, and consider these questions to consolidate your learning.

- *Who should attend the strategy discussion?*
- *Should the case progress to a child protection conference? Why?*
- *Who should attend the child protection conference?*
- *What category should the children be made subject of a child protection plan?*
- *Who should be in the core group?*

Comment

The strategy discussion should be attended by the social worker, social work manager, consultant paediatrician assigned to Faye in hospital, safeguarding lead from her school and police.

It is right that the case progress to a child protection conference as Faye has suffered a significant injury because of parental negligence and alcohol use.

The child protection conference should be attended by the same professionals as identified for the strategy discussion, including the child protection chair and parents. Faye has suffered an injury and therefore should be registered under physical harm.

The core group should be attended by those actively involved, including alcohol services.

Public Law Outline and Care Proceedings: key social work actions

Cases are escalated into The Public Law Outline and Care Proceedings frameworks when there are concerns that a child or young person is at risk of suffering significant harm. These frameworks take the safeguarding concerns into the legal arena, and solicitors become involved in safety planning and case planning for the child or young person.

Please refer to Chapter 6 where we discussed the difference between Public Law Outline (PLO) and care proceedings; however, in summary, PLO is the pre-court process, and care proceedings are going to court.

REFLECTIVE QUESTION

Does a case have to go through Public Law Outline before it goes into Care Proceedings?

Comment

This will be determined by the level of immediate risk of harm the child is assessed to be at. As a standard of practice, a Local Authority should always be transparent with a family about the identified safeguarding concerns and what needs to happen to achieve change, and families should be given an opportunity to change throughout Local Authority involvement. A Local Authority may issue care proceedings when either no change has been achieved within the PLO process or if the risks are assessed to be so high that the child's safety and well-being requires immediate issue. We will consider this further in the following case examples. As you read these, consider which framework is more appropriate, Public Law Outline or immediate issue of Care Proceedings?

CASE STUDY

A Local Authority receives a referral from the Court. The children live with their mother. Their father is seeking a Child Arrangements Order for the children to live with him. This is contested by their mother who alleges the children will not be safe as the father does not understand their medical needs. A medical report completed within the Private Law proceedings identifies concerns around Fabricated and Induced Illness by the mother. Following the referral, the Local Authority complete their own safeguarding enquiries and make similar findings.

- *Should there be immediate issue? Explain your reasons.*

Comment

There is a high risk of immediate harm and it is appropriate to make an application for immediate removal.

CASE STUDY

A family has been known to Children's Services intermittently for five years. The concerns are around neglect of the home conditions and children's needs, and domestic violence within the parent's relationship, now separated. The children have been subject to a children protection plan on two previous occasions. Mother has made changes in the past to come off plans but is unable to sustain changes. She has obtained a non-molestation order against the father, which is seen as a protective measure, but continues to contact him for support with managing the care of the children. The children are now on their third child protection plan. This plan has been going on for eight months with no evidence of change assessed.

Reflective question

- *What should happen? Explain your reasons.*

Comment

The children are not assessed to be at immediate risk of harm as parents are separated reducing the risk of witnessing frightening adult behaviours. We know that the mother has some capacity to make improvements when there is a high level of scrutiny. Therefore, it is appropriate for the Public law Outline to be initiated and for the family to be given a final opportunity to demonstrate change.

Key actions required when you have a concern that a child is suffering significant harm

There are several key actions you might take if you are concerned that a child is suffering significant harm.

- *Discuss escalating concerns with your supervisor or team manager* and jointly decide on the next steps required to keep the child or young person safe. Remember, safeguarding is everybody's responsibility. Your responsibility is to raise escalating concerns, and to do this timely.

- *Seek agreement for a legal planning meeting* when it is agreed a child is at risk of suffering significant harm. A senior social work manager needs to be kept informed about 'high risk cases' and needs to give agreement for a Legal Planning Meeting.

- *Trigger a legal planning meeting.* Follow the local process for requesting a legal planning meeting. This will differ from Local Authority to Local Authority, but usually involves completing a form which sets out the reasons why a legal planning meeting is being requested.

- *Legal planning meeting:* The purpose of a legal planning meeting is to seek legal advice on whether threshold has been crossed, i.e. has the child suffered significant harm, and what steps should be taken to keep the child or young person safe. It is a meeting for the Local Authority to decide what actions they will be taking. The family are not involved in this, although might be aware the meeting is taking place. A legal planning meeting is attended by a local authority solicitor, the allocated social worker and senior manager. In a legal planning meeting, the social worker will be required to present the case including the history of past and current concerns, the harm the children are suffering and the support that has been offered to date. The social worker should have a view on what should happen to keep a child safe. The Local Authority solicitor will advise on threshold, and whether Public Law Outline or Immediate Issue should be undertaken, and what appropriate orders should be applied for.

Public Law Outline

If the outcome of the legal planning meeting is to initiate the Public Law Outline process, you will be required to do the following:

- *Send out a letter before proceedings.* Most Local Authorities will have a standard template. All letters should set out what the main safeguarding concerns are, what support has already been provided and what assessments will be expected within the Public Law Outline process. It should have the date of the PLO meeting and provide the family with a list of solicitors who are registered as children and family law practitioners, who can represent them in the meeting.

- *Hold a pre-proceedings meeting.* The pre-proceedings meeting is a formal meeting, attended by the local authority solicitor, senior social work manager, the allocated social worker, the child's mother and father and their respective legal representatives. The meeting discusses the main safeguarding concerns and sets out assessments and work to be undertaken in improving safety and outcomes for the children.

- *Timescales:* the Public Law Outline process lasts around three months. There should be a mid-way review meeting to monitor progress. If no progress is made at the end of twelve weeks, the Local Authority may seek advice on issuing care proceedings. In exceptional cases, this timescale can be extended.

Care Proceedings

If the outcome of the legal planning meeting is to initiate care proceedings, you will be required to do the following:

- *Complete initial statement, care plan, chronology and genogram.* These documents must be prepared and submitted to the Local Authority legal team who will then make an application to the court. The social work team in consultation with legal team should be clear about what their interim care plan is, i.e. where should the child live in the interim, what contact the child should have with key persons and what assessments are necessary to help reach final decisions about the children (see Chapter 6).

- *Case management hearing:* At the first hearing, the court will decide what should happen to the child or young person in the interim, i.e. is it safe for the child to remain in the parent's care or is interim threshold met for separation. If so, where can the child live and which placement will cause least disruption and emotional turmoil to the child. Interim separation is only granted if the court finds grounds that the child's immediate safety requires it. At the case management hearing, the court will direct what assessments need to be undertaken to allow the court to make final decisions and by when. Within all court hearings, the legal representative does the speaking. The role of the social worker is to give advice on the disputed issues, i.e. where the child should live, why an assessment should be undertaken, what are contact recommendations, etc.

- *Timescales and assessment phase:* any directed assessments, either by experts or social workers, must be undertaken within the timescales set by the court. The Public Law Outline process sets out that all cases should be completed within twenty-six weeks to prevent drift and delay for children and young people.

- *Continue to manage the case.* The social worker has responsibilities to continue to manage the case. This will include undertaking regular visits with the child or young person; referring parents to specialist interventions such as drug and alcohol support services, etc.; ongoing risk assessments and change work with the family. Continue to escalate or raise any safeguarding concerns.

- *Keep the guardian informed:* Children are allocated a children's guardian to represent to the court what they want to happen, and to make assessments and recommendations to the court on what is in the child's best interests. It is important to keep the guardian informed of case developments that impact on the safety and well-being of the child.

- *Prepare Final evidence:* At the end of the assessment phase, the Social worker needs to present to the court their final care plan, what their ongoing concerns are, how they feel the child can be safeguarded and prevented from suffering further harm and how the child can achieve permanence.

- *Being prepared to give oral evidence in Final Hearings.* Refer back to Chapter 6 for tips on giving evidence.

Child Looked After: key social work actions

A child becomes 'looked after' either under a voluntary Section 20 agreement of the Children Act 1989 or when the Court decides a child is at risk of harm in a parent's care, and the Local Authority is granted either an Interim Care Order or Care Order.

Under Section 20 of the Children Act 1989 agreement, a parent retains his or her parental responsibility. A parent's positive and meaningful engagement with the Local Authority is required to ensure day-to-day decision-making for the child or young person.

An Interim or Care Order allows the Local Authority to share parental responsibility and make day-to-day decisions for the child.

For a child to come into care, there must always be agreement by senior social work managers. Whether it is a voluntary agreement or court directed, it is a significant change in circumstances for a child, and senior management involvement in decision-making and case planning is required to ensure it is in the best interests of the child and necessary and proportionate use of Local authority resources.

The law sets out the Local Authority must ascertain the wishes and feelings of the child, the parents and any other person whom the Local Authority considers relevant, before accommodating a child.

Consider the following examples, and whether it is appropriate for the child to become looked after under S20 or Court Orders:

CASE STUDY

A girl is twelve years old. She is partially deaf blind with a diagnosis of autism and mental health difficulties. She displays challenging behaviours and struggles with transitions, for example, moving and settling in different safe environments such as between home, school and respite centres. The family are receiving a support package but continue to struggle to manage the girl's behaviours. This is consistent in different settings. It is assessed she needs a team of people to support and meet her needs.

Reflective question

- *What should happen?*

Comment

This girl has an extremely high level of need and although the parents are working positively with professionals and following professional advice, this girl is at risk at home, not because of safeguarding reasons but because of her additional needs. Joint assessment and care planning with health, education and social care is required in this case. A specialist education residential provision is likely to be required.

The law states that when a child is in a short break respite for longer than seventeen consecutive days or more than seventy-two days per annum, the child should be considered as 'looked after' and subject to Children Looked After procedures.

CASE STUDY

A fourteen-year-old boy makes contact to Children's Services and discloses he does not want to live at home as he is being hit by his father and treated differently to other family members. Parents are interviewed. They no longer want to look after him.

Reflective questions

- *What should happen?*
- *What factors need to be considered when making decisions around whether this boy should be accommodated under S20 or Court Orders?*

Comment

There is suggestion that there is physical and emotional harm to the boy. The parents are stating they do not want to look after him and are likely to agree to a voluntary S20 Agreement for the Local Authority to look after him. The Local Authority will not hold parental responsibility. What needs to be assessed and weighed up is whether the parents will work with the Local Authority to ensure day-to-day decisions are made for the boy.

CASE STUDY

A family has been known to children's services intermittently for ten years. Two children have previously been removed from parent's care. Parents have in the past worked with child protection and child in need plans to end children's services involvement. There are current concerns that children are directly witnessing domestic violence, one child has sustained a bruise likely to be caused by an adult (but disputed by parent), the family are at risk of being evicted due to antisocial behaviour and the children are being impacted emotionally.

Reflective question

- *What should happen?*

Comment

There is evidence that the children's physical and emotional safety is being harmed, and an application to the court is appropriate.

What are key social work responsibilities when placing a child in Local Authority care?

Coming into care means a child is changing their caregiver and this is likely to be disruptive and cause some emotional turmoil. The effects of this needs to be minimised as far as possible, and good placement matching is critical to successful and stable placements.

Every child is unique, and the law sets out that a child's religious persuasion, racial origin and cultural and linguistic background must be considered and matched where possible. When matching, the following additional factors should also be considered to prevent the least disruption to the child as possible:

- Who are the people important to the child and how often will there be contact; what is the impact of geographic distance of placement to home?

- Where does the child go to school; are they settled? Will they need to change school; what will the impact be?

- What are the needs of the child and experiences of the foster carer?

What are key social work responsibilities when a child becomes looked after?

When a child comes into care, the Local Authority becomes a corporate parent and has responsibilities to ensure the child's welfare is promoted and needs met.

The key social work responsibilities that a social work must undertake are as follows:

1. **Notify the relevant person/team within your Local Authority that the child has been placed:**
   This is to ensure the child is allocated an Independent Reviewing Officer (IRO). The role of an IRO is to ensure that the child's needs are met whilst in care, and that there is no drift and delay in care planning and decision-making for the child or young person.

2. **Placement planning meeting:**
   This meeting should happen within five working days of a child being placed. This is attended by the social worker, the foster carer and the supervising social worker. The purpose of the meeting is to ensure there is a handover of the child's needs and how these needs will be met whilst the child is in placement. For example, what are the provisions for their health, education,

emotional and behavioural well-being and contact. Agreements around hair-cuts, piercing, etc. might be discussed. The expectations of the foster carer should also be discussed and agreed, i.e. will there be requirements to supervise any phone calls, etc.

3. **Arrange an initial health assessment:**
    Every child coming into care should have a health assessment. The first health assessment should be completed within twenty days to allow the report to be shared within the first Child Looked After review. For children under five years of age, reviews should happen every six months. For children over five years of age, reviews should take place yearly.

4. **Statutory visits:**
    The law sets out the timescales for visiting children in care as follows: The first visit should take place within one week of being placed. For the first year, children should be seen within every six weeks. Thereafter, if the child is settled in placement, visits can take place every three months.

    When children are in care and subject to care proceedings, visits should take place every four weeks.

5. **Statutory Children Looked After Reviews:**
    The first statutory review should take place within twenty days of a child becoming looked after. The next review is held within three months; and thereafter every six months. It may be necessary to hold a review if there is placement breakdown or change in placement.

    A child looked after review is chaired by the IRO. The meeting should be organised by the IRO, but the allocated social worker has responsibilities for informing the IRO who the involved professionals are and who should attend this meeting. The attendees of a Children Looked After review usually include: the social worker and team manager, the mother, the father, the foster carer, the supervising social worker, key worker from education, key worker from health and the child—where appropriate. The meeting should not lose focus from the child or young person. This is not a meeting to discuss safeguarding concerns but rather how the child's identified needs, including contact, can be met and to ensure the child's needs for permanence are being progressed without drift or delay.

    The social worker has responsibilities to write a report in advance of this review and to share this with the IRO, parents and child where appropriate.

    The IRO will write up and distribute the meeting outcomes.

6. **Personal Education Plan:**
    A Personal Education Plan is a plan to ensure a child in care reaches their learning outcomes. It should be started within ten days of a child coming into care and is reviewed termly.

    A Personal Education Plan is usually triggered by the Virtual Schools Team, and the social worker should ensure this team is notified when a child is placed.

The Virtual Schools Team offers support to children in care with regards to their education needs. This may include, for example, finding a school placement if a child needs to change schools.

The Personal Education Plan meeting is chaired by the Designated Teacher, and short- and long-term targets for the child, as well as what support is needed to enable the child in meeting these targets, are discussed, and agreed to support the child in achieving their educational outcomes. A child in care is allocated a monetary budget to support any identified learning needs. Discussions on using this in the child's best learning interests should take place. For example, if they are behind age-related expectations in maths, extra 1:1 tuition could be purchased to bridge the gap.

The attendees of a Personal Education Plan meeting include: the social worker, the designated teacher, representative from virtual schools, the child (for all or part of the meeting), the foster carer and where appropriate the parent. The person caring for the child should attend, and where it is not appropriate for the parent and foster carer to attend together, arrangements to include and involve the parent should be made.

Chapter summary

In this chapter, we have explained the key social work tasks when managing cases under differing frameworks. We have put together a quick reference guide to use as a memory aid to promote effective practice.

Child in Need checklist

Assess that the child is in need of support	
Arrange first Child In Need meeting	
Record meeting/update risk assessment	
Distribute minutes	
Visit child/undertake direct work four to six times weekly	
Carry out any interventions/signposting for support services	
Arrange next Child in Need meeting four to six times weekly (repeat steps)	

Child protection checklist

Strategy meeting	
Complete Section 47 enquiries: • Section 47 checks • Follow up on actions from strategy meeting • Formally record outcomes of the S47 investigations	
Request Child Protection Conference	

Ensure report for the Child Protection Conference is completed and shared with the family and conference chair in advance of the meeting	
Complete statutory child protection visits	
First core group meeting	
Record meeting/update risk assessment	
Distribute minutes (repeat steps)	

Pre-proceedings checklist

Legal planning meeting—outcome to follow PLO process	
Send out a letter before proceedings	
Hold a pre-proceedings meeting	
Provide specialist interventions/support/update risk assessment	
Mid-way meeting	
Final meeting	

Care proceedings checklist

Legal planning meeting—outcome to initiate care proceedings	
Complete Initial Statement, Care Plan, Chronology and Genogram	
Case Management hearing	
Complete any directed assessments, i.e. parenting assessment; make any referrals, i.e. for Family Group Conference/specialist assessments. Refer to court order to be clear of what actions you are required to do	
Continue to manage the case	
Update the children's guardian when necessary	
Prepare your final evidence and care plan	
Issues resolution hearings	
Final hearing	

Children Looked After checklist

Notify the relevant person/team within your Local Authority that the child has been placed	
Placement planning meeting (within five working days)	
Ensure any arrangements for contact are in place	
Ensure any arrangements for the child's needs are made, such as arranging transport to/from school	

(Continued)

(Continued)

Arrange an initial health assessment (within twenty days of becoming looked after)	
Statutory visits • First visit within one week of placement • Thereafter six weekly	
Statutory Children Looked After Reviews. • First review with in twenty days of becoming looked after; second review within three months • Thereafter, six monthly	
Personal Education Plan • To be started within ten days of coming into care • Reviewed termly	

References

ADCS (2014) *Social Work Evidence Template (SWET)*. Available at: https://adcs.org.uk/care/article/SWET (accessed 17 March 2020).

Baginsky, M, Eyre, J and Roe, A (2020) *Child protection conference practice during COVID-19: rapid consultation*. Available at: https://www.nuffieldfjo.org.uk/resource/child-protection-conference-practice-covid-19 (accessed 17 March 2020).

Bride, B E, Radey, M and Figley, C R (2007) Measuring compassion fatigue. *Clinical Social Work Journal*, 35 (3), pp. 155–63.

Bronfenbrenner, U (1979) *The ecology of human development*. Cambridge, MA: Harvard University Press.

Calder, M (ed.) (2008) *Contemporary risk assessment in safeguarding children*. London: Russell House Publishing.

Choate, PW and Engstrom, S (2014) The "Good Enough" parent: implications for child protection. *Child Care in Practice*, 20 (4), pp. 368–82. https://doi.org/10.1080/13575279.2014.915794

Cunningham, M (2003) Impact of trauma work on social work clinicians: empirical findings. *Social Work*, 48 (4), pp. 451–59.

Department for Education (2014) *Managing risks and benefits of contact*. Available at: https://foster-ingandadoption.rip.org.uk/wp-content/uploads/2014/02/DfE-Topic-15-managing-risks-and-benefits-of-contact_final_09_07_14.pdf (accessed 17 March 2020).

Department for Education (2015) *The Children Act 1989: guidance and regulations, volume 2: care planning, placement and case review*. Available at: https://assets.publishing.service.gov.uk/government/uploads/system/uploads/attachment_data/file/441643/Children_Act_Guidance_2015.pdf (accessed 17 March 2020).

Department for Education (2017) *Family safeguarding Hertfordshire: evaluation report*. Available at: https://assets.publishing.service.gov.uk/government/uploads/system/uploads/attachment_data/file/625400/Family_Safeguarding_Hertfordshire.pdf (accessed 17 March 2020).

Department for Education (2018) *Working together to safeguard children*. Available at: https://www.gov.uk/government/publications/working-together-to-safeguard-children–2 (accessed 17 March 2020).

Department for Education (2019) *Children Looked After in England, (including adoption), year ending 31 March 2019*. Available at: https://assets.publishing.service.gov.uk/government/uploads/system/uploads/attachment_data/file/850306/Children_looked_after_in_England_2019_Text.pdf (accessed 17 March 2020).

Department for Education (2020) *Outcomes for children in care*. Available at: https://assets.publishing.service.gov.uk/government/uploads/system/uploads/attachment_data/file/875529/CLA_Outcomes_Main_Text_2019.pdf (accessed 17 March 2020).

Department of Health, Department of Education & Employment, Home Office (2000) *Framework for the assessment of children in need and their families*. London: Stationary Office.

Devilly, G J, Wright, R and Varker, T (2009) Vicarious trauma, secondary traumatic stress or simply burnout? Effects of trauma therapy on mental health professionals. *Australian and New Zealand Journal of Psychiatry*, 43 (4), pp. 373–85.

Figley, C R (1995). Compassion fatigue as secondary traumatic stress disorder: An overview. In C R Figley (ed.), *Compassion fatigue: Coping with secondary traumatic stress disorder in those who treat the traumatized* (pp. 1–20). New York, NY: Brunner/Mazel.

Grant, L and Kinman, G (Eds.) (2014) *Developing resilience for social work practice.* pp. 232.

Grant, L and Kinman, G (2020) https://local.gov.uk/sites/default/files/documents/workforce%20-%20wellbeing %20social%20care%20-%20Community%20Care%20Inform%20emotional%20resilience%20guide.pdf

Kellett, J and Apps, J (2009) *Assessments of parenting and parenting support need: a study of four professional groups* (PDF). York: Joseph Rowntree Foundation. (accessed 17 March 2020).

Knight, C (2010) Indirect trauma in the field practicum: secondary traumatic stress, vicarious trauma, and compassion fatigue among social work students and their field instructors. *The Journal of Baccalaureate Social Work*, 15 (1), pp. 31–52.

Laming (2003) *The Victoria Climbie inquiry. Report of the inquiry by Lord Laming. Report Cm573 (5).* London: Stationary Office.

Laming (2009) *The protection of children in England: a progress report.* London: Stationary Office.

London Safeguarding Children Partnership (n.d.) *Best practice guidance for child protection conferences.* Available at: https://www.londoncp.co.uk/best_prac_cpc.html#8.1-who-should-attend-a-child-protection-conference (accessed 17 March 2020).

Ludick, M and Figley, C M (2016) Toward a mechanism for secondary trauma induction and reduction: reimagining a theory of secondary traumatic stress. *Traumatology*, 23 (1), pp. 1–12.

Maclean, S and Harrison, R (2015) *Social work theory: a straightforward guide for practice educator and placement supervisors.* Staffordshire: Kirwin Maclean Associates.

Marmot, M (2004) *Fair Society, Healthy Lives.* Available at: https://www.instituteofhealthequity.org/resources-reports/fair-society-healthy-lives-the-marmot-review/fair-society-healthy-lives-full-report-pdf.pdf

Maslach, C (2017) Findings solutions to the problem of Burnout. *Consulting Psychology Journal: Practice and Research*, 69 (2), 143–52. https://www.anesthesiallc.com/images/eAlertsSource/Finding-solutions-to-burnout-Maslach-CPJ-2017-3.pdf

McFadden, P (2015) *Measuring burnout among UK social workers: a community care study.* pp. 146. https://www.qub.ac.uk/sites/media/Media,514081,en.pdf

McFarlane, A (2021) *Message from the President of the Family Division: The Road Ahead 2021.* Available at: https://www.judiciary.uk/announcements/message-from-the-president-of-the-family-division-the-road-ahead-2021/ (accessed 17 March 2020).

Miller, W R and Rollnick, S (2013) *Motivational interviewing: helping people to change.* New York, NY: Guilford Press.

Ministry of Justice (2021) *Family procedure rules.* Available at: https://www.justice.gov.uk/courts/procedure-rules/family/rules_pd_menu (accessed 17 March 2020).

Munro, E (2008) *Effective child protection* (2nd ed.). London: SAGE.

Munro, E (2011) *The Munro review of child protection report: moving towards a child centered system.* London: Department of Education.

Munro, E (2012) *The Munro review of child protection. Final report – a child-centred system*. London: Department of Education.

Northamptonshire Children's Social Care Services. (2013) *Strengthening Assessment & Intervention*. Workshop Handbook. Strengthening Practice Programme.

NSPCC (2020) *Gillick competency and Fraser guidelines*. Available at: https://learning.nspcc.org.uk/child-protection-system/gillick-competence-fraser-guidelines (accessed 17 March 2020).

NSPCC (2021) *Statistics briefing: looked after children*. Available at: https://learning.nspcc.org.uk/media/1622/statistics-briefing-looked-after-children.pdf (accessed 17 March 2021).

Ofsted (2021) *National Statistics Main findings: children's social care in England 2021*. Available at: https://www.gov.uk/government/statistics/childrens-social-care-data-in-england-2021/main-findings-childrens-social-care-in-england-2021 (Updated 16 July 2021).

Pines, A and Maslach, C (1978) Characteristics of staff burnout in mental health setting. *Hospital and Community Psychiatry*, 29 (3), pp. 233–37.

Prochaska, J and Di Clemente, C (1982) Transtheoretical therapy: towards a more integrative model of change. *Psychotherapy: Theory, Research & Practice*, 19 (3), pp. 276–88.

Quinn, A, Ji, P and Nackerud, L (2018) Predictors of secondary traumatic stress among social workers: supervision, income, and caseload size. *Journal of Social Work*, 19 (4), pp. 504–28. https://doi.org/10.1177%2F1468017318762450

Rutter, L and Brown, K (2020) *Critical thinking and professional judgement for social work*. Thousand Oaks, CA: SAGE.

Schon, D A (1983) *The reflective practitioner: how professionals think in action*. New York, NY: Basic Books.

Social Work England (2021) *Speaker's corner – Monday: social work week*. [online video]. Available at: https://youtu.be/mcNcp1ow8XQ (accessed 15 June 2021).

Teater, B (2012) *Curriculum guide—Social work intervention methods*. Available at: https://www.basw.co.uk/system/files/resources/basw_104913-2_0.pdf (accessed 17 March 2020).

Trevithick, P (2012) *Social work skills and knowledge: a practice handbook*. pp. 432.

Trowler (2018) *Case for clear blue water*. Available at: https://www.sheffield.ac.uk/polopoly_fs/1.812158!/file/Sheffield_Solutions_Clear_Blue_Water_Full_Report.pdf (accessed 17 March 2020).

Turnell, A and Edwards, S (1999) *Signs of safety: a safety and solution-oriented approach to child protection casework*. New York, NY: W. W. Norton.

Turner, A (2020) *Coronavirus: 75% of social workers feeling more negative about their work-life than last year, survey finds: community care*. Available at: https://www.communitycare.co.uk/2020/12/11/coronavirus-75-social-workers-feeling-negative-work-life-last-year-survey-finds/ (accessed 17 March 2020).

Winnicott, D W (1965) *The maturational processes and the facilitating environment: studies in the theory of emotional development*. Madison, CT: International Universities Press.

YouGov (2020) *A report on the social work profession for Social Work England*. Available at: https://www.socialworkengland.org.uk/media/3326/yougov-the-social-work-profession.pdf (accessed 17 March 2020).

Index